LIVING WATERS

*Being Bible Expositions and Addresses
Given at Different Camp-Meetings and to
Ministers and Christian Workers on
Various Other Occasions*

*Introduced with the Author's Experience in
Spreading Holiness*

by
Sheridan Baker

Author of
A Peculiar People

"Living waters shall go out from Jerusalem." —Zech. 14. 8
"Whosoever will, let him take the water of life freely." —Rev. 22. 17

SCHMUL PUBLISHING COMPANY
NICHOLASVILLE, KENTUCKY

Cover image copyright: <a href='http://www.123rf.com/profile_michaklootwijk'>michaklootwijk / 123RF Stock Photo</a>

Published by Schmul Publishing Co.
PO Box 776
Nicholasville, KY USA

Printed in the United States of America

ISBN 10: 0-88019-600-9
ISBN 13: 978-0-88019-600-0

Visit us on the Internet at www.wesleyanbooks.com, or order direct from the publisher by calling 800-772-6657, or by writing to the above address.

Contents

PUBLISHER'S PREFACE

SHERIDAN BAKER WAS ONE OF the best known revivalists of the nineteenth century, noted for his business acumen coupled with a free-flowing financial liberality. Instrumental in the National Association for the Promotion of Holiness, a highly successful pastor, church planter and college president, he was also a businessman who made and gave away several fortunes.

Along the way he found time to prove his worth as an editor and writer. But he was best known for his skill behind the pulpit. Like his spiritual forebear, John Wesley, he deliberately chose his words and styled his sermons to be easily understood by every one of his listeners.

In this volume he discusses the life of holiness in practical terms. He delves deeply into the attainment of entire sanctification, warning of the sidetracks that may divert seekers from the true blessing. But he does not stop with a cleansed heart. He urges the sanctified, both the newly purified and the veteran saint, to press forward, to grow in grace.

Here is a masterful exposé of the Second Blessing

by one who insists we must seek God himself rather than his blessings. The blessings will come along as a matter of course.

—D. CURTIS HALE
Publisher, 2017

PREFACE

THE AUTHOR HAS BEEN solicited at various times, and by different brethren conversant with such matters, to put into book-form and give to the public selections from his Bible Expositions and Addresses. He has heretofore refused upon the ground that nearly all the important truth that would appear in them can be found in the literature of Christian holiness already published and circulated in the Church. To this it has been replied that the various methods of stating truth are quite as important to readers as the truth itself; and that the literature upon any subject treated is complete just in proportion as the different authors or teachers shade it by their peculiar modes of thought and statement. This and the author's disability at present for more active work, have led him to collect, select, and revise the choice of his Expositions and Addresses, and prepare them for publication in the shape here given.

These discourses were addressed to audiences before they were written and given to the papers and periodicals which first published them, with the exception of the

Introduction and a few articles which now appear in print for the first time. Most of the illustrations and familiar forms of speech suited to public audiences have been omitted, and verbiage suited to readers rather than hearers has been adopted. The principles and truths of the originals, however, have been so carefully preserved that the reader who heard them given to audiences will readily recognize them in their present printed dress.

To save a division of the book, short and appropriate scriptures have been prefixed to the Addresses, and they have all been arranged under the general head of "Expositions," and divided into chapters; and these chapters have been, so arranged that the first twenty, it is hoped, will be edifying to general readers, and especially helpful to seekers of the great salvation. The next ten or twelve were mostly prepared for and addressed to annual and district conferences, ministerial associations, and other conventions of Christian workers, and were intended to be helpful to these classes of religious laborers. The remaining chapters were prepared and used for building up in faith and holiness all classes of Christians and in all the different stages of spiritual life.

It was the supreme ambition of the author, in the original preparation of these Expositions, to bring out the mind of the Spirit, the literary character being quite a secondary consideration. Now, as he reads them over with a view of compiling a book, he is not entirely blind to their literary defects; nevertheless, he commits them to this form and sends them forth to a Christian public, hoping when he has passed away, an event most likely at no great distance in the future, he may continue to speak to a few upon the great theme which has been the subject of his thoughts and the joy of his heart for more than seventeen years.

—S.B.
Coshocton, Ohio

INTRODUCTION

THE AUTHOR'S EXPERIENCE IN THE WORK OF SPREADING HOLINESS

IT IS THE AUTHOR'S CONVICTION that he cannot prepare, nor can he get another to prepare, a more suitable introduction to the great theme to follow than to give a summary of his experience in the work which called forth the expositions and addresses which compose this book. This, then, he will proceed to do in the use of the first person singular.

My efforts to teach and press the subject of holiness upon the churches are coetaneous with my ministry. Very soon after my conversion, which took place in my twenty-third year, while a senior at college, I felt the need of holiness of heart, and commenced to seek it. As soon as my probation expired I was received into full connection, licensed to preach, and assigned to work under the presiding elder. At the ensuing session of the Annual Conference I was received on trial, and sent as junior preacher upon a circuit embracing eight Sunday and five week-day appointments. While traveling this, my first circuit,

I frequently fasted, prayed, and groaned for full salvation. In the meantime I became acquainted with Wesley's counsel to his preachers, to preach sanctification "constantly, explicitly, strongly," if they had the experience, and, if not, to preach it till they obtained it. Taking this advice I prepared a few sermons on the subject, gathering the material largely from Upham's *Interior Life*, and something from other treatises upon the same theme.

These sermons I preached at most of the appointments on my large circuit with comfort to myself and, I think, with profit to my brethren. For years after these sermons were staple with me on other charges. They had been prepared with great care, and were suitable for any field of labor, and especially for opening protracted meeting work. Some of these discourses I would frequently use on such occasions, and would urge the brethren to the altars of prayer to seek a deeper work of grace and a preparation for the work of soul-saving, but never to entire sanctification as set forth in the preaching. I had not reached this myself, nor did I know how to grasp it or lead my flock into its possession. The discourses, however, were greatly blessed of God in arousing the membership and keeping alive an interest upon the subject in my own mind. But though this course was followed for about twenty years I did not get into the experience myself, nor have I any reason to believe that any of my membership did. And, while my ministry during these years was regarded by my brethren as quite successful in revivals and making accessions to the churches, I look back upon it with sadness that so little was done in really building up the Church of God in faith and holiness. I now see that all this time I lacked a complete equipment for my work, I had not "tarried" until I was endued with power from on high and prepared for the great business of the gospel ministry, which, the apostle says, is "for the perfecting of the saints, for the work of the ministry, for the edifying of the body of Christ."

There came a time, however, when I got into a furnace of desire seeking holiness, and while I was in that state I noticed my hearers greatly moved under my preaching, and believers were led to see their great need of deeper spirituality and were led to reach after it. I was in this state of desire for some two months or more, and preached frequently during that time and always with marked effect upon the hearers; yet I knew of no one entering the experience, though I knew some commenced to seek. But as soon as I declared that the blood of Jesus Christ cleansed me from all sin; that I "reckoned myself dead indeed to sin, but alive unto God," and preached holiness from the stand-point of experience, immediately others were aroused to seek and soon gave testimony that they found. While all were aroused many were offended, and apparently driven away from the subject entirely. In my ardor and zeal I presented the theme in colors too bold and in forms too radical for many of my brethren of the laity, and some, I have feared, were injured in their spiritual life rather than benefited by my early efforts.

I soon learned that it was one thing to preach holiness as a theory, or as one of the doctrines of the Church, and quite another thing to preach it as an experience and for the purpose of urging it upon believers. The very identical sermons that were received with applause when preached as a doctrine merely were condemned by some when preached and urged as an experience. In their doctrinal dress they were pronounced beautiful, philosophical and scriptural, but in their dress as an experience they laid bare the heart, aroused opposition, and were pronounced by a few as schismatic discourses calculated to disturb and divide the Church. Those members, however, who were "hungering and thirsting after righteousness," and longing for all the mind "which was also in Christ Jesus," and who, consequently, were ready for the crucifixion of self and wanted to be nailed to the cross and get clear of the self-life, received these sermons with as much joy and gladness as if they had been directly "from the excellent glory." It was supreme delight to see these precious souls drink in the truth and rush to the altars of the churches as seekers of full salvation as soon as the opportunities were given. Of course they soon found and testified to the fact, and this induced others to waive their opposition to the doctrine and seek the same grace. Many, however, became so set in their feelings against the work of spreading holiness, either because they were repelled by the manner in which the subject was presented, or led into hostility by the great enemy, and their own native carnality, that they have never become friendly to the cause.

I learned, after some time in the work, that the Saviour's statement to his disciples, "I have yet many things to say unto you, but ye cannot bear them now," contained matter of great practical importance. After I got the impression that I might be too precipitate in my movements to lead the churches into a better religious state, I proceeded more cautiously in introducing the matter of holiness. I would commence the ten-days' meetings, which I was then holding through the churches, by a discourse or two upon the necessity of advancing in spiritual life, and get the membership committed to this by rising to their feet, or by coming forward to the altar for prayers. After an exercise or two of this kind, and testimonies on the same line, I would advance a little and ask them to definitely seek such a manifestation of Jesus to their hearts as would make them joyous and happy, give them freedom in speaking upon the theme of salvation, liberty in other religious exercises, and give them power to work in the meeting for the salvation of others. I found very few in all the churches that I visited as an evangelist who would refuse to make effort to advance in spiritual life and seek a preparation for Christian work. And when these efforts were continued a day or two, and they began to hunger and thirst, nearly all were ready to listen to what any person might have to say on the matter of entire sanctification.

With this caution in introducing holiness very few rejected the doctrine, and the body of the membership in many places sought the experience. And just in proportion as I have been enabled to carry out this policy in my work has been my success in leading the membership into the joys of full salvation. I have been called to labor in churches so disturbed and excited by incompetent teachers and by the mistaken conduct of professors of holiness that there was no chance to cautiously introduce the subject. I would find myself at once in the midst of a conflict awakened by an unwise presentation of the theme— a presentation in the forms most offensive to a formal membership and to feeble brethren not prepared to receive it. The only thing to be done then was to take up the subject in the form in which the people were discussing it and disengage it from what was false and erroneous, and present it in its true scriptural light. But often some had become so perverted and prejudiced that they would hear no explanation, and class all that was true with the errors that had poisoned them.

One of the most embarrassing things met with in my early labors was what, perhaps, may be styled the different types of holiness exhibited by the professors of this grace. I would meet persons quite prominent in some places as laborers on this line who seemed to make little of fastings, humiliations, and self-abnegations— who seemed to me to have an easy-going, self-indulgent type of holiness; who seemed, nevertheless, to be filled with love, peace, joy, and the other graces of the Spirit, and who were well received in their work by the mass of church members. When I would meet with these, so loving, so pure, so happy, so well received, I would wonder whether I had not allowed too much legality to creep into my spirit and life, and I would find myself taking on a somewhat milder type of holiness in my labors than I was wont to have. Soon, however, I would be persuaded that my religious state was suffering loss, and I would resume my wonted course.

Next I would meet with persons of an opposite character. They would cry out and spare not; they would lay bare the sins of the churches and the people in a most unmerciful manner; they would stir whole communities into a state of excitement in a short time; and they would gather to altars of prayer all the excitable, inflammable and radical characters in the church, and would soon have numbers in the experience of the great salvation. When I would meet these I would wonder whether I had not too mild a form of holiness to be the most effective; and my naturally radical make-up would readily take on more or less of this style. For awhile I would find myself handling sharper weapons than formerly, but with some recoiling of my finer feelings and with some disappointment at seeing the better and more reliable membership shrinking from my labors. I was not long, however, in discovering that I must take no man or set of men as patterns, but must look steadily to the Man of Nazareth, walk with him, and take on my own type or whatever type he put upon me. By so doing I was viewed by one class as dangerously radical and by the opposite class as dangerously conservative; but I was at rest, and in the enjoyment of what I believed to be the maximum of my power for usefulness.

When I first commenced to accept invitations to go

abroad and hold ten-days' meetings for the promotion of holiness such gatherings were novelties, and attracted preachers and people for many miles around. A preacher would occasionally arise in the meetings and openly oppose the doctrine preached and the efforts made for the sanctification of the Churches, but would invariably, before sitting down, insist on a deep spiritual life. I would not attempt a refutation of his positions, and thus open debate, but would restate what he had said of the necessity of deep spirituality, and call upon all who had not the Christian experience described by the brother to gather around the altar of prayer; and thus turn to good account whatever I could of what had been said. By adopting this course, the only course that seemed to me calculated to glorify God and aid in the work, these brethren soon tired in their opposition and either fell in with the work or went to their own charges.

Many would come great distances to these meetings for the purpose of seeking the grace which they learned would be held up for acceptance, and would announce their purpose at the first service they attended. Some of these would get alarmed as soon as they saw what it was about to cost them, or what their consecration must embrace, and would leave for home. Others, who had more carefully counted the cost, found the object of their pursuit and returned to their homes happy in God and with purposes to lift up the light among their brethren. Occasionally a person, who left without the grace sought because of its cost, would get so alarmed after reaching home that he would return, face the crucifixion and get gloriously saved. Now and then some official of the church in which the meeting was held, who felt that he had rights there which some others had not, would get contrary and stubborn, and go home to spend a sleepless night in repenting and calling upon God for mercy and would return next day shouting along the highway.

In the early years of my labor upon this line I received invitations from preachers and official boards who had no clear conception of what they were doing. They had heard of great religious excitements at other places where I labored, and they wished something of the kind in their churches, and hence extended the invitation. When I could accept, and commenced work at the time appointed, some were painfully disappointed to find that instead of preaching some wonderful sermons to move the public I commenced by reading the Scriptures and making some plain comments setting forth the necessity of personal communion with God. This over, I would ask the preacher and members to go to the altar with me for a season of prayer, and then for testimony as to what each one judged to be his own spiritual need. So displeased have I seen the good, but mistaken, brethren that had I not already been assigned to lodgings I could have found no place among them for entertainment. But, with one single exception through all these years, in a day or two they would become reconciled to the mode of work, the Church be filled with interested listeners, and generally the altars occupied by seekers of pardon and purity. Then the warm shaking of hands became so hearty and so abundant that, being a feeble person, I have had to dodge the courtesy and ask to be excused from accepting their invitations to the enjoyment of their hospitalities. At the close of the ten days I would have to leave these warm greetings to meet an engagement at some other place, where I would feel another chill at the commencement of the work.

The most desirable places to labor on this line have been college towns. In all our institutions of learning there are numbers of young men preparing for the ministry who ardently desire all the spiritual help they can get to prepare them for their life-work. Hence they have always attended upon my labors and readily fallen in with the work of holiness. They have rushed to the altars of the

Church for prayers by the scores, and in some places a hundred or more of these Christian students have professed perfect love during a ten-days' meeting. In my first visits to such towns, and witnessing the sanctification of so many young preachers and the zeal with which they would testify and labor, I would predict that the next decade was destined to witness a revolution in our churches on the subject of holiness. I assumed that all these young men would be faithful, and commence their ministry and continue it with this fullness of the Spirit. But before my prediction was fulfilled some of these became muddled in their views and experience at the theological schools; others were advised by the older brethren to be extremely cautious in preaching and urging the subject upon the churches; and others became alarmed as they saw that in some sections of the work a profession of holiness and preaching it with a view of leading believers into the experience were bars to the better class of appointments. Hence many of these, several hundred young preachers, have become as silent upon the matter as their fathers were. Deluded boys! They do not see, what I have clearly discerned in my work, that while this evasion of responsibility may open their way more rapidly to the popular pulpits it will also greatly hasten their descent from these places by and by, to say nothing of the painful failures in soul-saving which they must face and the awful sin that will confront them in the judgment. There are hundreds of preachers in the Churches to-day who have fallen into mental decay and spiritual death, and who have been forced into superannuation long before the time, because of their disloyalty to holiness, or to Christ, the embodiment of holiness. Had they stood up squarely for this grace, maintained the fullness of the Spirit, been true to their convictions, and labored cheerfully where such loyalty to God might have placed them, instead of being housed away in an unhappy mood, their labors would now be sought by the churches, and they would be realizing what the Holy Ghost says of such characters, "They shall bring forth fruit in old age; they shall be fat and flourishing."

Another source of pain to a person laboring for the sanctification of believers is the manifest disqualification of some churches to nurse and build up in faith and holiness those whom he has led into the blessed experience of full salvation. He leaves the societies in which he has labored with the sad conviction that the fruits of his toil will not be properly gathered, and that some, possibly many, happy in the faith of inward purity, will soon be miserable in the loss of this gracious state. Even in many of the churches whose pastors join the members in seeking and finding this experience this painful event will take place. The pastor will soon hear after the evangelist leaves that some member of the official board who did not fall in with the work, or some prominent sister who does not long for deep spirituality, and who has become uneasy and condemned for spiritual leanness, thinks that quite enough has been said upon the subject of holiness, and that something else ought to take precedence for awhile. The pastor, yet unskilled in the management of such emergencies, concludes it would be wise to keep silent for a season upon the sanctification of the church— the very thing he ought not to do while this official member or influential sister is under awakenings. At this point gentle perseverance in holding up the grace of holiness will lead awakened members to accept the experience or to take themselves out of the way of the pastor and give him an open field for the work of God. But dropping at this critical moment the great, "central idea of Christianity," and "the perfecting of the saints," the primary purpose in giving to the Church "apostles, prophets, evangelists, pastors, and teachers," the Spirit is grieved, coldness comes upon both pastor and people, and nothing more is heard from the pulpit upon the subject. Thus the good work dies out, except in the hearts of a few faithful persons who now seem to annoy rather than delight their brethren.

The case is sadder still in those societies which exclude from their services the work of getting believers made perfect in love, and whose hungry members go abroad to find the experience. These newly Spirit- baptized souls go home to their brethren all aglow with love, and zeal to save others, and commence to tell the story of their deliverance and urge on others the same grace. The brethren cannot bear this, and counsel them to silence, or something else which these Spirit- enlightened persons know they must not do. Then commences a breach which continues to widen till sad work takes place. The brethren who have tasted perfect love would not lose it for the world, and they see to take the course advised would subject them to this disaster. Hence they place themselves in an attitude to resist all such danger, and they are consequently regarded by those who do not understand them or their situation as insubordinate to the regularly-constituted authorities of the church. With no one to counsel in whom they have confidence these sanctified ones blunder along till they lose their sweetness and love, and take on what has been called "sour godliness," and are ready for almost any mischief.

There is another painful form of the Church's inability at present to care for her entirely sanctified children, which occasionally comes to the views of one whose spiritual discernment enables him to rightly estimate such things. A pastor with this experience and aggressive in the work will lead the body of his membership into the possession of perfect love, and quiet all opposition to the doctrine and experience, in the course of a year or two on the same charge. A few of the more wealthy and aristo-cratic members, who do not wish to be spiritually-minded, will not fall in with the pastor and their breth-ren in the holiness work; but, seeing the church prosper and the public generally in sympathy with the preacher and his faithful helpers, they keep quiet until another pastor, who knows nothing experimentally of the holi-ness movement, takes charge of the work. Then they tell him of the sad state of things as they see it; and he, being Inclined to the same view because of inexperience in this specific work, instead of feeding the holy people of the charge speaks so discouragingly of the movement that the weaker are hushed into silence and the stronger are driven together for mutual support in the trial. Satan then soon finds an entrance, the clan revolts, and the holiness movement is charged with the damages done. After a year or two the preacher reports the society about free from the annoyance and in a state of peace and rest! He has unwittingly freed that church from the "central idea of Christianity " and the "grand *depositum* of Methodism" which some faithful pastor spent two or three years to introduce and establish!

Holiness must be fed with proper aliment, or it will die just as surely as justifying grace; and did our churches treat regeneration and the witness of the Spirit as some of them do entire sanctification there would scarcely be a vestige of spirituality in all the land. Some preachers think that although they do not make a specialty of urging holiness upon the churches they nevertheless preach it, and their sanctified members ought to be satisfied and feed upon what they preach, which they are sure is the unadulterated gospel. Nothing, however, short of the genuine experience of holiness, kept fresh by frequent anointings of the Holy Ghost, can provide that heavenly seasoning and fragrance in preaching which purified hearers crave in their spiritual food.

After seventeen years of experience in this work, and with my eyes open upon what is passing among our churches, I am ready to accept as well-established principles and facts certain propositions which I will now state.

First, perfect love must be enjoyed by those who would labor successfully for the spread of this grace. As mere hirelings and professional preachers cannot get sinners converted, or led into true spiritual life, neither can mere theorists lead believers into the bliss of the purified. This is confirmed by the experience of the universal Church of all the ages. In spiritual matters no one can lead another beyond where he has gone himself.

Second, testimony to the enjoyment of perfect love seems as necessary to success in spreading it as the grace itself. As a matter of fact those preachers who seem to enjoy it, who can preach the doctrine correctly, but who have embraced the error that they should say nothing about their personal enjoyment of the grace, meet with no success in leading their people into the experience. What a terrible mistake— concealing from their brethren the richest thing they know about the Gospel!

Third, prudence, discretion, and divine wisdom appear as necessary as the grace itself, and the confession of it, to eminent success in leading the churches into holiness. Hence the divine direction, "Look ye out among you seven men of honest report, full of the Holy Ghost and wisdom, whom we may appoint over this business." Many feeble Christians are unable to bear the strong meat of the gospel, and must be carefully and gently prepared before it can be safely offered to them. Some religious societies have been so thoroughly poisoned, in various ways, upon the subject of entire sanctification that the preacher who would be successful in introducing the doctrine and experience must first thoroughly disinfect the place before he proceeds to this work.

Lastly, nearly all the irregularities and fanaticisms

which I have found among professors of holiness have been occasioned by the incompetency of their religious leaders to counsel and instruct them. These leaders, not discerning the grace which these brethren professed, nor understanding the holy ardor and zeal which impelled their movements, knew not how to guide into proper channels and utilize this strange religious fervor, and hence saw no course to take with them but, some-how, to repress them. Thus by bad counsel and rebukes these sanctified ones were loosed from their moorings and driven out into open sea, where they made ship- wreck of their faith. While this will not wholly exculpate these apostates, the judgment day will reveal blood on other skirts besides theirs.

I

RIVERS OF LIVING WATER

He that believeth on me, as the Scripture hath said, out of his belly shall flow rivers of living water, (But this spake he of the Spirit, which they that believe on him should receive; for the Holy Ghost was not yet given; because that Jesus was not yet glorified.)— John 7. 38, 39.

THE FIRST VERSE of this scripture contains the language of Jesus, and the second, inclosed in parentheses, contains the evangelist's explanation of the Saviour's meaning. Taken together they bring to view certain great facts which all Christians ought to prayerfully study.

1. *There is a grace above and beyond that which comes to the heart through initial Christian faith.*— It is something answering to the perfect love or entire sanctification of the Methodist standards and apostolic letters. This comes to notice in the tenses of the verbs used by the Saviour and his expounder. Notice the wording; "He that believeth on me"— present tense— "out of his belly shall flow"— future tense— "rivers of living water." So also in the evangelist's explanation, "But this spake he of the Spirit,

23

which they that believe" — present tense— "should receive"— future tense. Hence, the believing mentioned
here and the flowing of the rivers are not simultaneous
events or concurrent facts. The believing, with its experience and grace, are present facts; but the flowing of the
rivers was to be a future fact depending upon the continuance of this present faith and loyalty. The thought of
continuity is an essential element in the Greek present
tense, and hence these expressions might be correctly rendered, "He that *continueth* to believe on me, out of his
belly shall flow rivers of living water. (But this spake he
of the Spirit, which they that *continue* to believe on him
shall receive.)" Hence:

2. *This higher grace is the heritage of believers only.*— It
depends upon loyalty for a greater or less length of time
in the lower phases of religious life and experience. It can
and has been objected to this view that what was true
and necessary with believers in the Saviour's day, in their
passage from the old to the new dispensation, is no longer
true and necessary under the reign of the Holy Spirit. It
was necessary for believers at the inauguration of the New
Testament dispensation, it has been said, and truly, too,
to be raised up to the plane of the new commandment;
but as the Spirit came at that time to abide in all his fullness, penitent believers may now receive him at once in
all his offices without the twofold experience of the earlier disciples. And it would be difficult to disprove this
hypothesis were it not for some of the records made in
the Acts of the Apostles, and the general experience of
the Church from that day to this. It is recorded that after
the reign of the Holy Ghost was fully established, and
the Gospel was preached under the full light of the Pentecost, the converts of Philip at the city of Samaria were
led into the pentecostal grace by the subsequent labors
of Peter and John. So the converts of Apollos at Ephesus
were inducted to the higher experiences of Christian life

by the Apostle Paul. And so the converts of eighteen centuries have had to find some Joshua to lead them into the Canaan of perfect love.

3. *This higher grace is the Holy Spirit in his purifying and empowering offices.* — The evangelist said, "But this spake he of the Spirit, which they that believe on him should receive," using the capital S in writing Spirit, showing that he meant that divine personality known in the Scriptures as the Holy Ghost. The disciples spoken of here as "they that believe on him " had already received this Spirit in his regenerating and adopting offices, but were to receive him in the higher offices just named. Hence the Saviour said to them, shortly after the utterance of the text and before the Pentecost, in speaking of their acquaintance with the Spirit and what they were to know of him in the future, "Ye know him, for he dwelleth with you, and shall be in you." The "know him" and "dwelleth with" they had, but the "shall be in " they were yet to receive. They were yet to receive the fulfillment of the promise made through Ezekiel, that after a new heart and a new spirit were given and received "I will put my Spirit within you, and cause you to walk in my statutes; and ye shall keep my judgments, and do them." This "Spirit, which they that believe on him should receive," was to destroy all worldliness and greed, to remove the dangerous heat of passion and feeling, to temper all the appetites and propensities, to sanctify all the plans of desire and ambition, to remove the fears of calamity and death, and to open up in the heart an exhaustless fountain of sympathy and love for the needy and perishing. Hence, out of their inner being were to "flow rivers of living water."

4. *This grace manifests itself in service and testimony.* — To perceive the force of the Saviour's language attention must be given to the symbolism which he uses. The Oriental hydrants and running- pumps of those days were

cut from stone and wood in the image of a human creature, and the water issued from the mouth of the image,
giving it the appearance of flowing from the belly. As these
images, standing at the side of the Roman highways, gave
forth continued streams of water, because of a subterra-
nean connection by pipes with a fountain high above
them on the mountain-side, so believers, possessed of the
pentecostal grace and standing by the highways of life,
and having a hidden connection by faith with the infinite Reservoir of light and love and power, send forth constant streams of warning to sinners and encouragement
to believers. Let it be noticed that these streams are not
rivulets, but rivers; that they do not come forth under the
pressure of religious obligation, but "flow" under the
drawings of Christian privilege; and that they are not
turbid and muddy, but clear and limpid — "living water." It is the overflow of the heart that reaches others.
The Saviour said to his disciples in speaking directly of
this pentecostal experience, "Ye shall receive power, after
that the Holy Ghost is come upon you; and ye shall be
witnesses unto me." There is not much witnessing until
the pentecostal grace is received. It requires the incoming of the Comforter to fill the heart, liberate the spirit,
loose the tongue in testimony and warning, and start the
flowing of living waters."

5. *This grace is receivable upon the condition that Jesus
Christ be enthroned in the believer's supreme thought and
affection.* — "The Holy Ghost was not yet given; because
that Jesus was not yet glorified." Before the Holy Spirit
could descend in his fullness, inaugurate his reign in the
earth, establish the New Testament Church, and put in
motion the forces which were to produce universal righteousness, it was necessary that Christ should ascend and
be glorified at the right hand of the Father. So, before the
Holy Spirit can establish his reign in believers, they must
exalt Jesus above their business, their families, their dear-

est interests, and their own lives, and enthrone him upon the highest seat of the affections. No believer may expect the gift of the Holy Ghost until he brings to pass in his own heart that glorification of Jesus which took place in the third heaven, as the necessary condition of the original Pentecost. And a failure to do this on the part of believers now necessitates the record in the "book of remembrance" concerning thousands upon thousands of church members, "The Holy Ghost is not yet given; because that Jesus is not yet glorified." Wrestling Jacob did not receive the Comforter until he quit his struggling, forgot his trouble with Esau, dismissed the matter of a blessing, and asked for the *name*— the nature and being— of the strange Wrestler. "And he blessed him there" is the statement of what then took place.

Finally, This grace is free to all believers, and is confined to no particular class.— "*He* that believeth on me," whether rich or poor, learned or unlearned, high or low in social position, male or female, with wide or narrow opportunities for good, old or young in years— "HE that believeth on me, as the Scripture hath said, out of his belly shall flow rivers of living water." Does any one say that this language might apply to the rich, the eloquent, the learned, and those of great capacities and opportunities for doing good, but to apply it to believers poor and ignorant and confined, is extravagant and wild? Let such a person settle the question with the great Teacher, who knew what he said, and knew his words would be subjected to this criticism. Let him remember that the Saviour is speaking of unseen things, and things that do not address themselves to the carnal reason. He said of the widow's two mites that they were more than all the gold put into the treasury of the temple on that great day of gifts, and the last eighteen centuries have been proving the truth of his utterance. So eternity will prove that that feeble and circumscribed believer, with the constant real-

ization of the pentecostal grace, sent forth, unconscious
to himself and unsuspected by others, "rivers of living
water." Glory be to God for these wonderful possibilities
of our faith!

II
PHYSICAL AND SPIRITUAL CLEANSING

Having therefore these promises, dearly beloved, let us cleanse ourselves from all filthiness of the flesh and spirit, perfecting holiness in the fear of God. — 2 Cor. 7, 1.

THE PROMISES REFERRED TO in the text are named in the closing of the preceding chapter. They are promises of sonship and the divine indwelling upon the condition of separation from the sinful and the unclean. The persons addressed were believers, and hence were called "dearly beloved." They were most solemnly urged to seek a purified nature and to live a purified life. The language of the text supposes a few facts which now will be briefly noticed.

1. *Believers may not be entirely purified.* — Many persons seem to have great trouble with the notion that conversion does not necessarily imply entire cleansing. They cry out in surprise, Can God do a partial work? If he converts a soul is not the change perfect? Does it not dishonor God to suppose that when he converts a soul an additional work is necessary to complete the reconstruc-

tion? To these and many other questions of the same import it may be answered that it is not God's plan to do the entire work of salvation at once, or else conversion, and entire sanctification as well, would be coetaneous with awakening. But awakening precedes conversion, and for the same reason entire purification succeeds to conversion. And there can be no doubt that the completeness of the work in these several stages is measured by the degree of conformity to the conditions upon which God acts. He does, in every case, a perfect work up to the measure in which the conditions are met. When the Creator grows an oak upon a barren and sterile place it is as perfect as the conditions will allow, though it is scrubby, knotty, and almost worthless. When he grows the same tree on a fertile and suitable soil it is sound, tall, comely, and useful for many valuable purposes. Sometimes he grows the oak on a fertile soil, raising it to large and beautiful proportions, but from some unknown cause the beautiful creation is rotten at heart, hollow and useless. Among the animal creations there are many defective ones. Very few are perfect in symmetry and form, and fill the mold of perfect specimens of their kind. It is not strange, therefore, that there should be very great defection in the gracious work wrought in believers by the Holy Ghost, since this work is conditioned upon the believer's own conduct and faith. As the Creator makes all he can, or all that is possible, out of the tree growing in a sterile soil, so he works in believers all the possibilities of their condition. And because the conditions of entire purification are met in different degrees by believers, corresponding degrees or measures of grace are received, enjoyed and lived. Hence, the Christians addressed in the text, like the great body of believers to-day, were not entirely cleansed, but were earnestly urged to seek for it.

Another implication of the text is,

2. *Believers may now be entirely cleansed.* — Cleans-

ing is an eliminating process, a process of removing filthiness from the things cleansed. The process of covering up uncleanness and letting it remain in the thing called cleansed is foreign to the thought expressed in the Greek verb.

The verb used here is the same that is used in the gospels to express the cleansing or healing of the lepers. When lepers were cleansed their disease was not concealed by some covering, but was verily and truly removed from the system. Their flesh came again as the flesh of a little child, healthy and free from disease. So, when a soul is cleansed in the sense of the text, its pollution is not covered over by Christ's righteousness but is really and truly removed from its being and essence. Any imputation of Christ's righteousness which involves the idea of covering the sins of the sinner, and leaving him in his uncleanness, is not the true scriptural idea of imputed righteousness. The atonement provides for such a union with Christ that his life and purity shall flow through the believer, expelling all impurity and death, and assimilating him to the likeness and nature of Christ as the branch is assimilated to the likeness and nature of the vine. This is the Saviour's own figure.

Not only does the Greek verb signify a real cleansing, but, being in the aorist tense, indicating singleness of action, it gives no countenance to what has lately been called the repressive theory of entire sanctification. This theory holds that the carnal principle remains in the believer during life, and that entire sanctification is the grace that effectually and constantly holds the evil principles in repression. But the tense of the verb is fatal to this, as the tense expresses a finished action done once for all, and never to be repeated.

This tense is quite as destructive also to the Zinzendorf notion, that entire sanctification takes place at the time of conversion; and to cleanse ourselves after that means to continue clean, or to remain faithful. But the tense forbids the thought of continuity, and expresses the idea of a definite finished act. Had the apostle meant a continuous act he would have used the present instead of the aorist tense. Hence, the Greek scholar can see nothing in the wording of the text to support the repressive, or Zinzendorf theory, but sees an order for a specific, definite cleansing once for all.

There is a sense in which purified believers continue to purify themselves, but it is not expressed in this text. The believer puts himself at once, or by one act of faith, into the cleansing stream and is immediately made clean. He then continues in that stream, or continues faithful, and is kept clean. Purity is retained on the same condition that it is obtained; and to keep under the cleansing wave is to be faithful to the conditions of purity. The Saviour expresses this continual cleansing by the figure of abiding in the vine. Believers at once, or by one act of faith, become united to the vine and receive his life and purity, and, abiding in this vine, they continue to receive his life and bear his fruit.

The text assumes another fact that should be prayerfully studied; namely,

3. *Personal effort a necessity.* — "Let us cleanse ourselves." This language would seem to intimate that the work is entirely our own; but all readily understand it to mean that we have an important part to act in our cleansing. We are to meet the conditions upon which grace and mercy are pledged to do the work for us. First, there must be a renunciation of every thing that may be called filthiness of the flesh or spirit. Every bodily impurity, all misuse and treatment of the body, all mistreatment of the mind by reading or communications with others, all improper meditations and imaginings, all uses of the senses and instincts which would awaken impure thoughts and acts, and, indeed,

every thing, real and imaginary, that would corrupt must be abandoned forever.

Second, there must be a devotement of time, talents, money, influence, and every thing we possess, to the glory of God. All our dearest rights and life itself must be laid down at Jesus's feet and held subservient to the calls of humanity. This involves a divorcement of our affections from every thing lawful, so that nothing is done or enjoyed except in Christ. This disengagement of the affections from lawful things, so that they will not become the rivals of Christ, is a vital matter to purified believers, and is the point where they are most likely to stray. Having renounced every thing that is wrong, and devoted every thing that is good about us to the service of God, it only remains to believe that God, according to his promise, does now cleanse and purify. Upon the exercise of this faith the great transaction is done. The soul passes from a state of partial to a state of entire sanctification. The believer is truly cleansed from all filthiness of the flesh and spirit, and is now ready to perfect holiness in the fear of the Lord.

Another fact stated in the text is,

4. *Entire purity may be developed and matured.* — "Perfecting holiness in the fear of the Lord." Having obtained entire purity it is now to be carried into all the departments of life, and our habits are all to be adjusted to this gracious state, or, perhaps, more properly, the gracious state is to assimilate to itself all our habits of business and life.

This grace cannot be retained unless it is cultivated and used. It must control us in the treatment of ourselves; it must mold our spirit and conduct in the home circle; it must regulate our conduct with our neighbors; it must shape our course with our brethren in the Church, and it must mold the life which we live in ourselves. This continuous use of the grace is the "perfecting holiness" urged in the text; it is the "open face" by which we see, as in a glass, the divine image, and are changed from glory to glory as by the Spirit of the Lord.

III
Divine Strength for All

Be strong in the Lord.— Eph. 6. 10.

IT IS BOTH THE PRIVILEGE and duty of all to be strong in the Lord, and no one has a right to be spiritually feeble. Yet most Christians seem to think that they are irreversibly doomed, while here on probation, to spiritual defection and imbecility. But provision has been made that all may be strong, and, of course, all are placed under corresponding obligation to accept and seek the possession of the proffered grace. Hence the apostle most peremptorily orders the Churches "be perfect," "be strong," "quit you like men," and "be strong in the Lord and the power of his might." In the analysis of this subject note,

1. *All may be strong.*— The whole Church is addressed in the text, and this implies that the whole Church may be strong. All may not have much money, or great learning, or high social position, or any of the natural means of exerting an influence, yet all may have purity and be endued with power from on high. Many of the most efficient laborers of every age have been the most destitute

of the natural resources of power. Their great might has been the indwelling Spirit "of power, and of love, and of a sound mind." This cannot be found, where many seek it, in scientific study, or foreign travel, or any of the helps of mere intellectual culture, but may be found in union with Christ, which all, even the most lowly, may enjoy.

2. *All must be strong or criminal.* — The text and its parallels are mandatory, and no one can be inattentive to commands and be innocent. To seek the Spirit in such a limited measure as leaves us feeble is evident disobedience to the command to seek it in such a measure as will make us strong in the Lord. While, therefore, a weak faith, and consequent defective graces, are, as far as they go, pure and good, nevertheless, to continue or remain weak in faith and defective in the graces is very sinful, because God has provided better things, and, pressing them upon us, orders us to accept them. There is, then, no more apology for spiritual weakness than there is for lying, swearing, or any other form of disobedience to God's orders. Yet many point, it would seem, with a kind of spiritual pride to their weak faith and great unbelief as evidence that they are not over-righteous, or that they are not contracted in their views and feelings, or that they do not belong to the "holier-than-thou " class of Christians. How often we hear the expressions, complacently uttered, "O, my faith is so weak!" or "O, I am such an unbeliever!" Now, no one has a right to utter such sentiments, for no one has a right to be in such a state. It is just as honorable, really, and quite as consistent with true Christian character, to cherish and point to great worldliness, or great sensuality and lust, or great wickedness of any other form; for unbelief, which is always associated with spiritual feebleness, and measured by it, is the prolific parent of all the vices. To declare our sympathy, therefore, with

unbelief is to declare our acceptance of its fruitage, or our sympathy with vice.

To govern himself, to overcome the world and to accomplish the work here assigned him, the Christian must "be strong in the Lord and in the power of his might;" and this is within his reach, and a failure to grasp it is highly censurable.

3. *This strength is in the Lord.* — It is divine power put in motion by the creature's faith. "God is our refuge and strength." "The Lord Jehovah is my strength and song." When the Christian is filled with the Spirit there is a complete crucifixion of self, and he feels that his own strength is gone, and in the distinct consciousness of his own weakness his faith moves the Mighty Arm. It is at this point of experience that he can appropriate the apostle's language: "Therefore I glory in infirmities, in reproaches, in necessities, in persecutions, in distresses for Christ's sake; for when I am weak then I am strong." Many, at times, and with feeble purpose, seek this power under the mistaken notion that its possession will cause them to feel like spiritual giants, and make their work appear to others like the work of masters, or will enable them to do something that will excite the wonder of their fellows. But the very opposite of this is more nearly correct. In the possession of this power the Christian is not only conscious of very great personal weakness, but so complete is the death of nature that he is willing — and delays not — to do any work for the Master, big or little, great or small, popular or unpopular. And most persons need this power, not so much to qualify them for great work as to humble them down where they will be willing to do the little work best suited to their capacities, and which, after all, makes up the great work of every one's life. Possessed of the abiding Comforter, and baptized with his mighty power, the humble believer finds happiness more in doing the will

of God, whatever that will may be, than seeing results, however extensive and sublime.

4. *This strength is reached by faith.*— No amount of study, or travel, or labor of any kind that does not imply the requisite faith, will avail. Like pardon, regeneration, or any other degree of saving grace, it is attainable by faith alone, and is found only in connection with complete, unreserved consecration to God. Any defection in the consecration enfeebles the faith, and consequently the spiritual power which is always commensurate with it. The Saviour has said: "How can ye believe, which receive honor one of another, and seek not the honor that cometh from God only?" Consequently, if this power be sought to enhance our own reputation, or if the honor that cometh from others be consulted, or if the purity of our motives in any other way be vitiated, our faith will be too much enfeebled to grasp the prize. "The honor which cometh from God only " must be sought.

But whoever surrenders himself fully to God, and in all earnestness and sincerity asks the gift of power to glorify him alone, has a right to believe, irrespective of frames and feelings, that it is communicated to him; or rather it is his duty to believe it given to him, and has no right to doubt it, but should proceed to his work assured that, in proper time and in a proper manner, it will be manifested, or his belief, in some way highly satisfactory to himself, will be commuted into knowledge. For, notice again,

5. *This power does not always manifest itself to the human gaze.*— Not every one endued with this power, and conscious of its possession, is permitted to see its manifestations like D.L. Moody or Bishop Taylor. There are many obscure and silent workers, the manifestations of whose power will not appear till the light of eternity breaks upon them. The poor widow whose endowment of power enabled her to give all her living, though it was but two mites, did not do much in the sight of men, nor is

it likely she did much in her own view; nevertheless the Saviour decided that she did more than all those rich Jews who came up from the great marts of the world's trade and, on that memorable day of gifts, cast in of their abundance. That little act, of such magnitude in the Divine estimation as to give it an imperishable record in the Sacred Oracles, has been comforting the poor saints and enriching the Church for nearly nineteen centuries, and will continue to do so while time endures. No doubt the widow felt blessed in the deed, and was conscious of a power to cast herself and her living at the Redeemer's feet, but had no idea of the widespread issues and extensive bearings of the act until she was carried by angels into Abraham's bosom.

The Saviour says: "He that abideth in me, and I in him, the same bringeth forth much fruit." He does not say the moneyed man, the educated person, the person of great natural endowments "that abideth in me," but "he that abideth in me," whether rich or poor, whether lettered or unlettered, whoever he may be, and whatever may be his surroundings or opportunities, "the same bringeth forth much fruit." The great amount of fruit may not appear to men, but He who said, "The kingdom of God cometh not with observation " discerns it in the humble fidelities of the lowly, as well as in the widespread influence of the more conspicuous of the saints.

Instead, therefore, of pining away under regrets that we have not been more richly endowed, or furnished with better opportunities, let us seek power to be "faithful over a few things," and this will secure to us the "rule over many things;" all that will be conferred upon the more gifted. Glory be to God! though we may not do the great work of a Spurgeon or a Talmage, we may be endued with power from on high, and by humble fidelity to the trust reposed in us may rise to the same sublime heights in the Eternal Land.

IV
THE REASONABLE SERVICE

I beseech you therefore, brethren, by the mercies of God, that ye present your bodies a living sacrifice, holy, acceptable unto God, which is your reasonable service. And be not conformed to this world; but be ye transformed by the renewing of your mind, that ye may prove what is that good, and acceptable, and perfect will of God. — Rom. 12. 1, 2.

THE TEXT IS AN EXHORTATION to believers. The title, "brethren," used in the address, as well as the duty urged, prove that Christians are addressed. None can offer sacrifices to God but those who have first received Christ, and offer them through him. Hence it is not the work of a sinner, nor a penitent seeker of salvation, but the duty of a true believer that is brought to view.

Notice some of the points presented in the passage.

1. *The offerings required.* — "Present your bodies." Most likely the word "bodies" was used by the apostle to mean nothing more than the physical man, with its appetites, senses, and whatever else appertains to it, as the believer's

safety is most imperiled through these channels. If, however, the word was used by figure of speech to signify the whole man, physical, intellectual, and moral, the meaning is practically the same. The apostle evidently teaches through all his writings that Christians should hold themselves, and all they have, living sacrifices, holy, and acceptable unto God.

But do not penitent seekers of salvation make such sacrifice to God? And are not such offerings necessary to pardon and adoption? To these questions it may be answered: Penitents cannot be said to offer sacrifices to God, they surrender to God; they submit themselves to God and receive Christ as their Saviour, but do not in any scriptural and proper sense make sacrifice to God.

2. *The qualities required in the offerings.*— "Present your bodies a living sacrifice, holy, acceptable unto God." Supposing penitents should offer sacrifices to God, they could not offer such as are ordered in the text. Penitents are not recovered from the death in trespasses and sins, and cannot, therefore, offer a living, a holy, and an acceptable offering such as is required in the text, and hence are not the characters addressed.

Christians, however, having been raised from spiritual death, and having become spiritually alive and active in religious work, can present themselves living, holy, and acceptable sacrifices to God. Hence, Christians are the characters addressed, and the obligations imposed are the appropriate and necessary duties of justified believers.

3. *The manner of sacrificing.*— Properly appreciating "the mercies of God," believers are asked to *present* their bodies a living sacrifice. This indicates a voluntary and cheerful tender of all to God. This is very different from the unpleasant and reluctant surrender which a penitent makes in his abandonment of sin and acceptance of Christ.

The aorist tense of the original verb indicates a specific and finished action, done once for all, and never to be repeated. It indicates a tender of self such as is made in the marriage covenant, never to be revoked or to be repeated. It shadows forth an entrance into more intimate union and more endearing relationships with the adorable Redeemer.

Holy people speak of renewing their covenants with God, and repeating their consecrations; but, unless there have been violations of covenant engagements— a thing not contemplated in the wording of the text— such expressions can mean nothing more than reindorsements of these engagements. Another point to be noticed here is, that all this is declared to be,

4. *The reasonable service of believers.*— It is often objected by members of the Church that coming forward to the altar, or doing something of the kind as an act signifying the presentation of themselves as living sacrifices, holy, acceptable to God, puts them in a wrong light before the people. They think it is a declaration of lukewarmness, of backsliding, and of need of reclamation. In this they are very much mistaken. God's order to the lukewarm and to those in any degree backslidden is. "Remember whence thou art fallen, and repent, and do the first works." Such persons are not ready for the high and holy order of the text. None are ready for it but persons living in the clear light of justification, active Christians, holy Christians, Christians acceptable to the Church and to God, but needing an interior transformation.

To ask members of the Church, therefore, to do some act signifying that they do present their bodies a living sacrifice, holy, acceptable unto God, is to concede to them all the spirituality they claim— to concede to them a high state of justification— a state of readiness to enter a state of entire sanctification. To ask such persons to present themselves living sacrifices to God is to ask them to do a reasonable service, something becoming earnest Christians, something suitable to holy persons, something in harmony with the nature and inclinations of true believers. It is the reasonable service of Christians needing a deeper work of grace, or desiring an advance in Christian life. This service performed, the believer is ready for more advanced orders.

Many religious teachers stop at this point, separating the first from the second verse, and leaving the impression upon the hearers that the great matter to be reached is such a consecration to God that he will get all their time, talents, money, and service for the spread of his kingdom and glory. The objective point to be reached, however, is a state of the heart, the experience of purity, expressed by "proving what is that good, and acceptable, and perfect will of God." To reach this experience and inward state something more is to be done than what is named in the first verse; the direction of the second verse must be observed. Many overlook this entirely, as well as the objective point to be reached, in urging entire consecration upon the Churches. They see nothing but service to be rendered, while the great primary matter is inward holiness as a necessity to a complete New Testament experience in divine things. True and effective service will flow from this state, but is not brought directly to view in the scripture now under notice. That which should be especially emphasized in edifying and instructing believers from this passage is the necessity of heart purity. But to reach this more than the presentation of the bodies is mentioned by the apostle as necessary, and he proceeds next to press upon his readers,

5. *Nonconformity to the world.* — This shows where the complete abandonment of worldly habits and customs properly takes place in the divine arrangement of things. This order is not given to sinners, nor even to believers, until there is first a presentation of themselves as living

sacrifices, holy, acceptable unto God. They are ready then, and not until then, for a complete and eternal divorcement from all that is carnal and worldly. Hence all those societies and efforts to reform man, without leading him to the cross for a new nature, are radically defective. They are attempting to run the waters up stream, which can only be done by breastworks, and then only for a short season. The accumulated waters, soon breaking through the embankments, flow on in their old channels.

This command is to wholly consecrated Christians; and to ask women not in this state to change their style of dress, or men to change their worldly habits, is to cast pearls before swine; to excite their pity and ridicule, and to do them no good. They must first be converted, and then come into a state of entire consecration, and into a longing for all the mind that was in Christ. In this state of mind they are ready for the order, "Be not conformed to this world," and ready to receive the suggestions and help of their brethren in getting clear of the trappings, the glitter, and the follies of this world. The next, and a still higher order is,

6. *An inward transformation.* — This renewing of the mind, which renders divorcement from the world natural and easy, does not take place at conversion, as the apostle assumes in the text, and universal experience proves. It is a fact of experience that young persons, clearly converted, retain their old affinities for worldly pleasures and amusements. The power of the affinities, it is true, is broken, but they still exist. Older persons, clearly converted, have trouble with their self-will, their former worldliness, and their old tempers and evil dispositions; and the trouble continues until they are sanctified wholly. Hence the Scriptures teach believers to pray, "Create in me a clean heart, O God," and command them to cleanse themselves from all filthiness of the flesh and spirit as a post-conversion work and experience.

It will be seen that the believer is led by this scripture from doing to a state of being— from the active sphere of presenting himself a living sacrifice, holy, acceptable unto God, into the passive state of receiving a transformed nature. He is to "*be* not conformed to this world," but is to "*be* transformed by the renewing of the mind." This means that, the sacrifice once made, the subject of grace has nothing to do but claim his rights in the atonement and let the Holy Spirit purge from all that defiles. It means when the point of entire, unreserved, and eternal surrender is reached there is nothing to do but passively trust and wait; nothing but a heart-response to the Spirit, receiving him as the abiding Comforter to work out his sovereign will in the soul. Unnecessary struggling at this point, and a discovery of the error, produced those significant lines of a hymn now often sung:

"Long my yearning heart was trying
To enjoy this perfect rest;
But I gave all trying over:
Simply trusting, I was blest."

Interior purity and the divine indwelling are gifts, and must be simply received like other gifts, without labor or struggling when the point is reached where they are graciously tendered. The last thing to be noticed is,

7. *The experiences of this transformed nature.*— "That ye may prove what is that good, and acceptable, and perfect will of God." God's disposition or will toward his creatures is infinitely wise, and pure, and good. It is joyfully accepted by all pure intelligences; and men would count it a fearful disaster to change this will in any way when they come to see its benevolent aims and ends.

This transformed nature has such clear spiritual perceptions that they transmute all theory respecting the perfect will of God into real facts. That all things, however painful to the flesh, work together for good to them that love God is no longer problematical, or mere theory, but is demonstrated to the soul's consciousness. The universe and all its diversified parts now appear in their true light and relations as so many channels for the diffusion of happiness to sentient creatures, and especially to the saints. The revelation that "Eye hath not seen, nor ear heard, neither have entered into the heart of man, the things which God hath prepared for them that love him; but God hath revealed them unto us by his Spirit," has become a veritable experience. The deep peace, the celestial sweetness, and the heavenly rest, promised to the entirely consecrated and spiritually transformed, are actual realizations! Glory be to the Father, glory be to the Son, and glory be to the Holy Ghost! Amen.

V
CONSECRATION AND PURIFICATION

If any man serve me, let him follow me; and where I am, there shall also my servant be. —John 12. 26.

OUR SAVIOUR HAD JUST EXPLAINED the nature and necessity of his death by an allusion to a plain and universally known fact in the vegetable kingdom: "Except a corn of wheat fall into the ground and die, it abideth alone; but if it die, it bringeth forth much fruit." Had he not died, as the seed of humanity, the race could not have been preserved; and had he remained in the body he could not be seated upon the mediatorial throne and at the same time be present with all his people. But by dying, rising and ascending, he has so multiplied his glorified humanity that every believer may have an advocate with the Father, and a living personal Christ with him and in him all the time.

This death he next uses as the type of the sinner's regeneration. "He that loveth his life shall lose it; and he that hateth his life in this world shall keep it unto life eternal." Whoever is so much in love with this life that he holds it above discipleship with Christ shall lose his soul; but whoever holds it practically below this discipleship, so that he will suffer martyrdom rather than prove disloyal to his Lord, shall save his soul. Thus, to obtain regenerating and adopting grace the sinner must absolutely surrender his life to God; and any Christian profession and supposed gracious state costing less than this is spurious, and not sealed with the Holy Spirit of promise.

By the same death he next typifies the believer's entire sanctification. "If any man serve me, let him follow me; and where I am there shall also my servant be." These words set forth entire sanctification in both its branches, of entire consecration and entire purification, as a little study will disclose.

1. *Entire consecration.*— If any man serve me, let him follow me." After the experience of self-surrender and consequent incoming of spiritual life, as expressed in the verse immediately preceding the text, follows the duty of service and growth in grace. The divine orders to young Christians are such as these: "With purpose of heart cleave unto the Lord;" "Watch and pray, lest ye enter into temptation;" "If ye then be risen with Christ, seek the things which are above;" "Strive to enter in at the strait gate;" Mortify therefore your members which are upon the earth;" "Be ye holy;" "Be filled with the Spirit," and others expressive of religious activity and advanced Christian experience. So far as the element of service is concerned the Saviour sums all these orders into the crisp statement, "Let him follow me." To follow Christ is to engage in all the activities of Christian worship and work which the Lord assigns to each believer. It is to practically say, or act out, the Saviour's confession, "I came not to do mine own will, but the will of him that sent me." "My meat is to do the will of him that sent me, and to finish his work." It is to obey the apostolic order, "Whether therefore ye eat or drink, or whatsoever ye do, do all to

the glory of God." It is to sell and buy, to go and come, to labor and rest, to enjoy and suffer, and to be, to do, and to suffer everything else that the Lord may assign. None can do more than this, and nothing short of this will satisfy even the young Christian aiming to become Christly. Hence, in the divine order, the exercise of entire consecration follows in quick succession to the experience of regeneration, and is necessary to the preservation and development of spiritual life.

The young convert who will faithfully execute the above orders will soon discover something in his heart averse to such fidelity. He will find an inclination to neglect some clearly revealed duty, or a disposition to indulge in some pleasure or gratification of the flesh which he knows to be at variance with inward purity. In other words, he will discover, if correctly instructed by his religious teachers, the inborn depravity of his nature, and will hear the divine call, "Cleanse yourselves from all filthiness of the flesh and spirit, perfecting holiness in the fear of God." Just at this point in religious experience, for various reasons not to be stated at present, the great body of young converts, like ancient Israel at Kadesh, shrink from entering the Canaan of perfect love, and either abandon the Christian profession or go into a tread-mill use of the means of grace without any satisfactory spiritual life. The spiritual life imparted at regeneration dies out in the refusal to "follow on to know the Lord." A formalism sets in which greatly impedes the cause of true religion in the Church and gives a terrible meaning and application to the Saviour's words, "The publicans and harlots go into the kingdom of heaven before you."

Such a course is far from meeting the arrangement of Christ. He wants no slaves or unwilling laborers in his work. It is not service or patronage that he asks, but affection, fellowship, love. He asks for this consecration primarily to bring the believer into divine harmony with himself, that he may have communion with his Lord here and be united to him in holy and everlasting fellowship in the world to come. The matter of service is a secondary consideration, and is to be rendered not so much as duty but as privilege and pleasure. Hence, while the text urges an active life of religious work, it contemplates it as a delight in wedded union with Jesus. This inward state is expressed by the words, "Where I am, there shall also my servant be," as will be readily seen. Notice, then, that the text urges:

2. *Entire purity.*— Not to "be" with Christ is to be morally unlike him. When the Scriptures speak of sinners as far from God they do not mean distances measured by feet, inches and barleycorns, but by moral unlikeness. The distance is not geographical, for saints and sinners alike live and move and have their being in God. The exhortation, "Draw nigh to God, and he will draw nigh to you," does not mean a change in location, but in moral relations. A suppliant on the rings of Saturn, or on a fixed star millions of miles upward, would be no nearer his Maker than in any terrene position. To draw nigh to God is to throw off every thing unlike him, to take up and practice whatever is like him, and to look to him with a humble trust for a corresponding inward state. So, when the Saviour says, "Where I am, there shall also my servant be," he has no reference to place, but to spiritual union and fellowship. He means that the servant shall be in such inward harmony with him that service and communion will be supreme delight.

To reach this state the regenerated believer must follow Christ, in the law of death, to the cross, and submit to the utter extirpation of the self-life. Until this takes place there will appear, in the spirit and lives of even regenerated persons, a carnal principle in some form, and chiefly, perhaps, as a religious Ego, which vitiates the devotions and renders impracticable a true and scriptural obedience to the Saviour's expressed wish, "Where I am, there shall also my servant be." But, this crucifixion completed, the servant naturally and easily displays the meekness and gentleness of his Lord. Without a strain he imitates his Master in the prediction, "As a sheep before her shearers is dumb, so he opened not his mouth." He lives and walks and communes in blissful union with the adorable Bridegroom. This is what the Saviour desires and asks more than all service and sacrifice, and is the gracious state to which all scriptural consecration directly looks.

There has been in recent years a great awakening upon the subject of entire devotement to God, and all the pulpits are urging it upon the membership of the Church. But unhappily very little is said upon the necessity of entire purification, the great and most important matter in Christian life and experience. This is either unwittingly or intentionally overlooked, and the consecration urged expends itself in the mere externalities of religion. It is made to consist in what is called the work of the Church, including fairs, festivals, bazars and the like, rather than in devotion to God and his work of soul-saving. Hence there are thousands to-day in the different Churches who neither pray, testify, nor take any other part in spiritual worship, and who persuade themselves that they have no talent for such exercises, but have talent for other exercises in church work, such as managing sociables, conducting sewing societies, cooking at church festivals, gathering material for bazars, and other secularities. Thus, through the carelessness or ignorance of religious teachers, they are allowed to substitute these things for spiritual life, supposing they are doing the work of the Lord while they are in a state of unregeneracy and "without God in the world." There is, therefore, a terrible omission in insisting upon entire consecration without pointing directly to entire purity to which such consecration primarily looks.

But if mere service were the end to be reached entire purification should be pressed as a necessity to divine enduement for real Christian work. True, it utterly spoils a church member for some things called the work of God by the modern Church, but for true evangelism it multiplies the believer many-fold. His purity is felt wherever he goes; he scatters around him a heavenly fragrance that lasts; his spirit and demeanor are remembered and coveted by the good when he is far away, and he becomes in some sense omnipresent with all who know him. As he fills the prediction of Jesus, "Where I am, there shall also my servant be," he will, within the sphere of his personal activities, be with his Lord wherever there are the hungry to feed, the naked to clothe, the sorrowing to comfort, the perishing to save, and will have reached the maximum of his usefulness.

Finally, whether the expression, "Where I am, there shall also my servant be," be viewed as mandatory or predictive, it involves the promise of all the gracious help needed to reach this blessed communion. Whoever serves Christ in the sense of following him, or in the spirit of utter self-surrender, has the right to claim, indeed, it is his imperative duty to claim, complete deliverance from the carnal man and blessed union and fellowship with his glorified Lord. Such a believer is positively ordered to "reckon himself dead indeed unto sin, but alive unto God through Jesus Christ our Lord."

VI
THE TEST QUESTION

But whom say ye that I am? —Matt. 16.15.

THE SAVIOUR ASKED the disciples the question, "Whom do men say that I, the Son of man, am?" They answered, "Some say that thou art John the Baptist; some, Elias; and others, Jeremiah, or one of the prophets." We cannot suppose that he "who knew what was in man" asked this question for the sake of information, but for the purpose of introducing another of infinitely more importance to the disciples. It was of little moment what others believed or knew of Christ, but paramount what they themselves believed and knew. Hence, they are brought to directly face the question, "But whom say ye that I am?" Peter answered, "Thou art the Christ, the Son of the living God." Jesus replied, "Blessed art thou, Simon, Barjona: for flesh and blood hath not revealed it unto thee, but my Father which is in heaven."

The question in the text taken in connection with its associated facts, is highly suggestive. Some of these suggestions it is proposed to name and briefly discuss.

1. *Salvation is a personal matter.*— Our salvation is dependent upon our belief in Christ. What we believe Christ is to us personally measures our religious status. Hence, inserting and throwing the emphasis on the personal pronoun "ye" made the question a vital matter to the disciples. They had just told Jesus what others believed concerning him; now they are asked to state what they believed themselves, or, which is the same thing, to define their own spiritual state.

There is something in man which leads him to think much about the religious condition of others, and to form a judgment as to what that condition is. Most people can tell all about the piety of their neighbors and fellow-citizens, and seem to feel a greater certainty in the correctness of the judgment formed than in the judgment which they form of their own spiritual condition. Something seems to have been implanted in the original constitution of man leading him to look after his brother's spiritual interests, but the fall, which deranged his entire nature, perverted this into his brother's censor, or uncharitable critic. The text would call our attention away from others until we have applied the gospel square and plummet to ourselves and determined our own condition, and, in that light of careful investigation, adjusted our own relation to God. "Whom say *ye* that I am?"

2. *The spiritual state should be declared.*— Throw the emphasis on the word "say" and this becomes apparent. "Whom *say* ye that I am?" It is not enough to entertain certain sentiments or convictions concerning Christ, be they ever so correct; it is also necessary to declare those convictions. The Scriptures place a great deal of stress upon the open avowal of our attitude toward Christ. "Whosoever therefore shall confess me before men," says the Saviour, "him will I confess also before my Father which is in heaven. But

whosoever shall deny me before men, him will I deny before my Father which is in heaven." "With the heart man believeth unto righteousness, and with the mouth confession is made unto salvation." If we have no saving faith in Christ we should at once confess it, and seek salvation; or, if our faith does not save us to the "uttermost" we should confess that, and seek the purifying grace. As long as we conceal the state of our heart we are not likely, such is the divine arrangement, to reach a more satisfactory experience.

There are thousands in the Church, among both the ministry and laity, who are seeking, with considerable earnestness, power to do efficient work, or an unction fitting them for some special service, but who are unwilling to acknowledge their need of purity, and, consequently, make no advance in the pursuit of the coveted gift. Nor is it likely they ever will succeed till they come out squarely and acknowledge their want of clean hearts, and definitely seek personal purification. Then the power needed, possibly not the power coveted, will be communicated. As it would be a fatal error for a parent to grant a request from a disobedient child which would only be proper to grant to an obedient one, so to grant to those who refuse entire purity that unction and power which belong alone to a state of purity would put those at ease who ought to be disturbed, and would introduce discord into the harmonies of the universe. To ask God, therefore, to baptize us with the Holy Ghost and with fire, while we are refusing to put ourselves in proper attitude toward him and the truth, is to ask him to become a party with us in overthrowing the divinely-established order of things. O, my Christian brother, cease asking for power till you have cried to God for purity, and have been "made every whit whole."

If we have learned Christ as our all-sufficient Saviour, it is necessary, if we have to "say" what we believe concerning him, to declare this in order to retain the acquaintance. It is absurd to suppose that we can live in the highest and most intimate relationship with Jesus and disregard any of the tests of that relationship or refuse obedience to any of His requirements. "Whom say ye that I am?" is a question propounded as much to the highest as the lowest forms of faith; and a truthful answer is as much demanded from one as the other. Indeed, an evasive answer would be more inconsistent with the higher than with the lower experiences. Moreover, the faith in Christ which saves to the uttermost ought to be published for the purpose of encouraging others who are in a state of unrest and have not yet learned a better way. Thousands upon thousands, for the want of such testimony, are, today. groping in unnecessary darkness and bearing unnecessary burdens.

The question suggests also that,

3. *Christianity has her test question.—* From what has already been said it will be seen that the question is a test of faith; but there is something more definite and specific to be brought out of the text as a test question for our times.

Under the Old Testament, Bible religion had its test question, and whatever form it assumed at any period the answer involved the rejection of idol worship and the acceptance of the true God. Hence, a refusal to engage in the idolatrous worship of the Medo-Persian kings, and the persistent worship of the God of heaven, exposed Daniel and his Jewish brethren to the lion's den and the fiery furnace. Under the New Testament the answer to the question, whatever form it may take, involves the renunciation of all sin and the acceptance of Christ for what we understand he has engaged to do for us. This has exposed the believer to the loss of his reputation, to personal abuse, and the loss of life itself, in many parts of the globe, and in many periods of Church history.

During the incarnation and through apostolic times the

question under discussion took the form of the text, and the answer was suited to it. Hence, when Peter answered it as he did, the Saviour replied to him, "Blessed art thou, Simon, Barjona," and proceeded to state that the reason he was blessed was, God had become his teacher and helper in this matter. Hence, also, the apostle said, "No man can say that Jesus is the Lord, but by the Holy Ghost." These sayings of the Saviour and the apostle mean that no man, by his unassisted reason, could discern the Messiah of the prophets in the humble man of Nazareth, nor would he dare, at any time, to publish his discovery after it was made. Both the discovery and the publication of it required divine illumination and help.

"The Jews had agreed already that if any man did confess that he was Christ, he should be put out of the synagogue." For this reason a public confession of faith in Christ as a Saviour was attended with self-denial and self-abnegation, with all the mortification and cross-bearing, with all the renunciation and crucifixion, which are involved in a death to sin and self and a life hid with Christ in God. Hence the apostle John could say, "Whosoever shall confess that Jesus is the Son of God, God dwelleth in him, and he in God" — that is, such a confession at that time, and under those circumstances, was complete renunciation, complete consecration, and complete faith, and were followed by the incoming and indwelling of the abiding Comforter.

To answer this question in our day so as to involve the self-abnegation and crucifixion which precede conscious salvation the reply of Peter must be somewhat modified. To declare the man of Nazareth the Christ of the prophets, or the Son of God, is now no cross, is attended with no mortification, because it is the popular sentiment. Nor does it imperil a man's reputation or endanger his person to declare faith in Christ as a personal Saviour, pardoning his sins, and witnessing to the soul his adoption into the family of God. Such a testimony is now expected of all church-members, and no one is reproached for making it, if his life is thought to correspond with his profession. It was not always so. Not many years ago a confession of conscious pardon and the witness of the Spirit to the fact of adoption, through faith in Christ, was regarded wild and fanatical; and whoever gave such testimony was marked, suspected, and, in some places, abused. In the superior light of the last half of the nineteenth century this state of things has changed, and all who live anywhere near gospel requirements may express faith in Jesus as a personal Saviour, consciously pardoning his sin, without incurring the ban of society.

In the light of this age an answer to the test question requires us to come forward and declare Christ an all-sufficient Saviour, that he saves to the uttermost, that his blood *cleanseth us now* from all sin. This involves self-abnegation and crucifixion, because it is in advance of popular religious thought, and, consequently, incurs popular criticism and distrust.

Through all the ages of the Christian Church, and centuries before her organization, it was divinely announced, "I will turn my hand upon thee, and purely purge away thy dross, and take away all thy tin;" Wash me, and I shall be whiter than snow; yet, somehow, the revelation lay as a dead letter upon the inspired page. For the last few years, however, the Church has been awaking to her high privileges, and eminent divines and laymen of every branch of Zion are coming forward and declaring Christ a perfect Saviour, saving them personally, and now, from all sin, inward as well as outward. These facts indicate that God is calling his Church, every-where, and of every name and order, to this experience and testimony. In the light of the present age Christ must be confessed as a *perfect and all-sufficient Saviour*. Vacillating faith and perfunctory service will no longer answer.

VII
THE BELIEVER'S RECKONING

Likewise reckon ye also yourselves to be dead indeed unto sin, but alive unto God through Jesus Christ our Lord.
—Rom. 6. 11.

THIS SCRIPTURE IS AN ORDER to justified believers, and justified believers are Christians who are reaching after holiness of heart. It is the nature of evangelical faith to reach after God. True penitence reaches after pardon, pardon after purity, and purity after heaven. Truly justified persons, therefore, are reaching after entire sanctification, and to grasp it they are here ordered, instead of seeking it by works or growth, to claim it at once by reckoning themselves "dead indeed unto sin, but alive unto God through Jesus Christ our Lord." Hence those Christians who do not reckon themselves "dead indeed unto sin" must take another step before this death and life can take place. They must obey the text. Notice, then,

1. *The gracious state urged upon the believer.* — This state is denominated "dead indeed unto sin" and "alive unto

God," indicating both a negative and a positive phase. To be "dead indeed unto sin " is to sustain the same relation to it that the inhabitants of cemeteries sustain to the commerce, business, and bustle of this world. As their dust may be shaken by the heavy lumber-wagon as it passes by, or the locomotive as it thunders along its track, so may believers dead to sin be shaken by sin in the family, sin in the community, and sin all around; but they have no voluntary connection with it. To come into this state the believer must suffer the crucifixion of self, he must be nailed to the cross until the self-life becomes extinct and he is "crucified with Christ."

The Greek word rendered sin in this connection is *hamartia*, which is defined by Green "a principle or cause of sin; proneness to sin, sinful propensity," and, consequently, to be dead indeed unto sin is to be dead indeed to the proneness or propensity to sin; it is not only an abandonment of all sinful actions, but also the loss and absence of all dispositions to bad actions; it is not only a refusal to do wrong, but it is an inward aversion to, and a recoil from, all wrong-doing. As we reckon ourselves dead to the crimes of murder, robbery, theft, and felonies of all kinds; as it never enters our minds to commit such offenses, and as we view ourselves morally incapable of the like, so those who are "dead indeed unto sin" feel that "it is not in them" to do or approve whatever they believe our heavenly Father disapproves, however innocent men may judge these things to be.

There is a great deal that passes for death unto sin which is merely phenomenal, and, like that of the opossum when attacked by its enemy, it cannot stand the application of fire. The death urged here is such a deadness to self, to the world and to every thing offensive to God that it is no more moved to sinful action than a corpse is moved to resentment by insult and injury, or reciprocal laudation by flattery and praise. Holiness does not destroy our perceptions or sensibilities and render us incapable of seeing or feeling an insult, but it does destroy our tendencies to resent it; it does not destroy our susceptibility of being impressed by flattery, but it does destroy our disposition to drink it in and to be governed by it; it does not take away our desires for the necessaries of life, or for the means by which they are secured, but it does remove all undue love for them and all dispositions to seek these things through illegitimate channels, or to seek them with undue solicitude in lawful ways.

Just here theorists make bad work. An eminent modern commentator says, As a corpse is perfectly unsusceptible both in regard to outward things and internal sensations, so should the Christian be insensible both to the external excitements and the internal impulses to sin." One dead to sin is indeed insensible to internal impulses to sin, but, surely, *not insensible to external excitements to sin*. If this were so there could be no temptation to sin, and, consequently, the life of trial or probation must be at an end. The apostle used figures freely, and they must not be interpreted with too much exactness, or serious mischief is the result. Deadness to sin only is what we need, and not to temptation and other things belonging to a life of probation.

There is another element in this gracious state to be noticed, called "alive unto God." The original word rendered "alive" is a present participle expressing not only the living principle, but this principle in action; thus indicating that the believer, being purified, must next be filled with the Holy Spirit and started into channels of Christian activity. Some reckon themselves dead unto sin and come into a very quiescent state, but do not reckon themselves alive unto God, and thus come into the possession of the active element of holiness, and by this failure become disheartened and go back, or are greatly harassed by the enemy till they complete the reckoning and become alive unto God. To guard against this mistake and unnecessary delay the apostle orders the reckoning to embrace both the negative and positive sides at the same time, and earnest seekers very generally experience the cleansing from sin and occupancy of the heart by the Holy Spirit to be coetaneous events. Hence sanctified persons generally refer to a time when they received both purity and power, while a few refer to a time when they were cleansed from all sin, and to a later date, when they received the power or were baptized by the Holy Ghost. This diversity of experience depends, doubtless, upon the reckonings, some completing it in one act of faith, the others by two distinct acts at different times.

This life which succeeds to the crucifixion of the carnal nature, or a death indeed unto sin, may be called a life indeed unto God. As there is a spurious death unto sin which will not bear crosses, persecutions, and fiery trials for Christ's sake, so there is a spurious or merely phenomenal life unto God, that is made to appear like spiritual activity by money, church fairs, fashionable music, popular preaching, and other worldly stimulants. The life spoken of here, however, is one that acts by an inherent force of its own nature; it cannot keep quiet; it is ever restless to do service for God; it finds supreme pleasure in spiritual worship and work, and is "ready not only to be bound, but also to die for the name of the Lord Jesus." This is "the life more abundant." This is the spiritual condition to which all Christians should aspire and never rest till obtained. Notice next,

2. *How this gracious state is reached.* — It must be remembered that the scripture under consideration was addressed to justified believers who, from the nature of the grace already obtained, were reaching after holiness of heart. The apostle directs them to look away from works of righteousness and growth in grace to a simple act of faith which now claims the needed purity, which

now reckons the believer "dead indeed unto sin" — not *has been* dead, or *will be* dead, but who is *now dead* while he is consecrating himself, and believing, and reckoning, and will continue to be dead to sin while he continues the reckoning. In the execution of this order the believer will find that it has happened to him just as he has reckoned — he is purged from all defilement, he is made whiter than snow, and the Spirit witnesses to his spirit that "the great transaction is done."

The word translated "reckon" is a mathematical term, and means to count, to calculate, to reckon, and not to guess, to fancy, or to imagine. The Lord would have us be very sure upon this subject, and reach the conclusion with as much clearness and assurance as we would reckon the value of twenty yards of cloth at five dollars per yard. Though it is a moral problem, it has, like the arithmetical problem just stated, but two simple factors for data, and from these a conclusion can be reached with logical certainty. The first factor to be found, or question to settle, is: Does God offer to us such a state? And the second is. Do we accept the gracious tender? To settle the first we must look into the Bible, and as soon as we open its lids we find abundant promises that, on clearly stated conditions, we may be cleansed from all sin and saved to the uttermost. We look again and we find the commands to be wholly as plentiful as the promises, and when we come to the scripture which we are now studying we are struck with wonder to find that we are commanded to reckon ourselves now the possessors of this state. If, therefore, such a state is unattainable, the promises are a tantalization of believers, the commands are cruel mockeries, and the text and its parallels, which embrace both the promises and commands, are insults so gross that our language has no name for them. God, in good faith, offers his people full salvation now.

To complete the data for the reckoning in question it

only remains for justified Christians to accept the gracious tender. This involves a complete and entire consecration of themselves and all they have to God, and an acceptance of Christ for all he has engaged to do for his people here and hereafter. As soon as believers are conscious of such consecration and acceptance of Christ they are no longer at liberty to view themselves as unclean before God, for they are where divine mercy and grace are pledged to purify, and where they are ordered to call not that common or unclean which God has cleansed. They must, therefore, of logical necessity, if they would not make God a liar, view themselves, or reckon themselves, "dead indeed unto sin, but alive unto God."

Again, such an irreversible self-surrender to God implies ardent desires and intense longings for "the mind which was also in Christ Jesus;" but these longings and desires are the expression of character or moral condition already existent. Now, as longings to steal, or desires to murder, which only lack opportunity to execute the deeds, render their subjects thieves and murderers in the estimation of both God and man, so desires for purity, or longings to be like Christ, which only lack a knowledge of how to grasp the coveted grace, render their subjects pure in the Divine eye, and they are so entered upon his books. Hence, he who "calleth those things which be not as though they were" reckons them holy, and orders them to so reckon themselves, and upon executing this order that which existed in the Divine thought becomes a fact of experience in the hearts that make the reckoning.

There is another matter in this reckoning that ought not to be passed unnoticed. The tense of the Greek verb expresses the thought of a continuous reckoning as opposed to a momentary act done once for all; and this is vital to all who try to live holy lives. Many Christians take up the cross and pray with the sick, or bear part in public religious services, and for the time feel free and happy, but expect from former experiences to repeat this crucifixion when the same or similar duties are again to be performed. Thus they suffer a crucifixion at every step of their religious work; but if they were to reckon themselves "dead indeed unto sin" all the time, in the intervals of these exercises as well as when performing them, this crucifixion would not have to be repeated; the carnal man would remain dead according to the reckoning. Then, again, by overlooking this continuous reckoning the enemy will interject something that appears very much like the old Adam life; and if the subjects of this temptation fail just then to reckon themselves "dead indeed unto sin" they will get into serious trouble. If, however, at this juncture they keep up the reckoning, in spite of what might seem to them the return of the old nature, the enemy will be compelled to show his cloven foot, and the trouble will appear in its true light as a temptation of Satan.

Finally, this reckoning must be made in the name and strength of our Lord Jesus Christ. He has, by his passion and death, secured to us all our good, and were it not for this all our reckonings upon the matters named would be fruitless. Since, however, he has freed us by his death and graciously proclaimed that freedom, we should gratefully accept the boon by reckoning it ours. The slaves of the South were judicially free the moment the emancipation proclamation took effect, but only those slaves who reckoned themselves free at the time entered into the enjoyment of the freedom, while those who knew nothing of the proclamation, or, knowing all about it, did not appropriate it, continued to feel their bondage and their chains. So, when it is proclaimed from heaven, "Ye are dead, and your life is hid with Christ in God," believers must accept the statement as true, and appropriate it by viewing themselves as dead to sin, by talking of themselves as dead to sin, and by acting as those who are "dead indeed unto sin, but alive unto God." And as they think, and talk, and confess, and reckon, and act, so they will *find it to be* by the inworkings of the Holy Spirit and by his divine attestations of the fact to the heart.

Dear reader, are you a justified believer, are you sure of your pardon and adoption, are you longing for holiness of heart? If so it only remains for you to obey God and "reckon yourself dead indeed unto sin, but alive unto God through Jesus Christ our Lord." Don't ask, as many do at this point, How can I view myself as dead indeed unto sin when I do not feel so, but, on the contrary, feel the motions of sin stirring within me? Never mind what you feel or suppose you feel, but, in utter self-abnegation, obey God and reckon and confess yourself dead indeed unto sin, and cast all the consequences of this act of obedience upon God, who orders it. By so doing you will find yourself in the happy realization of all your heart craves and in a state of adoring wonder at the amazing simplicity of the plan of salvation, and reveling with delight in the wonderful wealth and sweetness of an uttermost salvation. Glory to the Father, glory to the Son, and glory to the Holy Ghost.

VIII
THE CONDITION OF TRUST IN GOD

Beloved, if our heart condemn us not, then have we con-
fidence toward God. —I John 3. 21.

B Y "CONFIDENCE TOWARD GOD" the apostle means
what we call faith in God. It is a sweet per-
suasion that he does now pardon, adopt, purify, keep, and love us freely for Christ's sake. Hence,
it makes him to us a Friend, a Father, and a Saviour. This blessed assurance, it is affirmed, comes
to us upon the condition that our hearts do not condemn us.

Among the suggestions of the text we may name:

1. *Confidence in God is conditional.* — Most of our good
is conditioned upon something. It seems to be a law of
the universe that we must take some antecedent steps to
reach every desirable thing. We must plow and sow and
gather the harvest if we would garner the products of the
earth. We must read and study and think if we would
enjoy a richly-stored mind. So we must observe conditions if we would enjoy the rest which confidence in God
brings to the soul.

2. *The condition is heart approval.*— "Beloved, if our heart condemn us not, then have we confidence." When does this take place? When have we the approbation of our own hearts? When we cease to do evil and learn to do well. When we consciously separate ourselves from every thing which we believe to be improper and sinful, and have accepted all the will of God; taken time, talents, reputation, our dearest rights, even life itself, and laid them down at Jesus's feet. We cannot then reproach ourselves for any delinquency, but must have the warmest approval of our own consciences. To reach this may require very close examinations into every department of our lives and habits, and repeated efforts at surrendering and yielding ourselves unto God. It may be necessary to descend in our examinations to the very lowest form of life we live, and see whether we cannot mend in the matter of eating and drinking, or waking and sleeping, and of working and resting; and then, carrying our investigations up through our intellectual, our social, our business, our domestic, and our private and inner life, separating from each whatever we may find objectionable. It may require also a carefully-constructed inventory of all we have, and a specific and formal transfer of each thing to God, before we can reach the consciousness of complete, unreserved, and eternal surrender. If all this can be done by one comprehensive sweep of the mind, and in a moment of time, all the better; only let it be done. But whatever difficulties may attend this adjustment of our relations to ourselves, to our fellows, and to God, the apostle assumes that it can be done, and done so satisfactorily that the conscience and heart are completely at rest upon the matter. Here at this point, and in this state, we have confidence toward God.

Another suggestion of the text is that,

3. *Confidence in God is a necessary sequence of heart approval*— "Then," says the apostle, "have we confidence

toward God." He does not say, Then may we have confidence, or, Then is it possible to have confidence, or, Then it is easy to have confidence, but, "*Then have we confidence toward God.*" We are where it comes to us of necessity; where, according to the laws of mind and the divine adjustments, we *must* have faith in God. In the absolute renunciation of all sin, and all forms of selfishness, and in the entire and absolute consecration of all we have and are to God, the soul can rest nowhere else but in God. There is nothing left upon which it can rest, and it necessarily passes from self and out of self into God. Of course, it is assumed here that the volitions are right; for it is not supposable in such absolute renunciation of self and consecration of all to God that the volitions are, or can be, discordant.

Up to the point of complete surrender the will has had nothing to do with the matter of actual trust in God, but only with the work of consecration, or the adjustment of our relations to God. The matter of actual trust does not come within the range of our volitions until the conditions of confidence are met, or until "our heart condemn us not." Every effort of the will to travel between two points by rail where there is no railroad is an absolute absurdity and failure, but after a road is completed such volitions are proper and successful. So, volitions to repose trust in God while in a state of alienation are absurd and futile, and are only proper and successful when we have gained the approbation of our own hearts and thereby met the conditions of trust.

The command, therefore, "Have faith in God," like such commands as, "Love your enemies," "Be ye holy," "Purify your hearts," "Be ye transformed by the renewing of your mind," are practicable only when we place ourselves where the Holy Ghost co-acts with our volitions and does his work in us, while we do our work with and through and by him. Hence the apostle would have us understand that when we have done our part, and placed ourselves where our heart cannot reproach us, the volitions being concordant, confidence in God is a necessary sequence.

Another implication of the text is,

4. *Confidence in God is not a constitutional peculiarity.* — Many persons speak of faith as something which arises from the peculiar make-up of pious persons, and of unbelief as having its origin in the same source. They apologize for their unbelief by a reference to what they suppose to be a constitutional obstacle in the way of trust in God. They say, O, we belong to the class of doubting Thomas. Thomas is referred to as a constitutional doubter; but for this there is no rational or scriptural warrant. Thomas was an impulsive fellow, and this led him, from some cause which did not justify the neglect, to absent himself from the first fellowship meeting held by the disciples after the resurrection, and he lost the benefits of that interview with the risen Lord. This was the secret of his unbelief. Had any of the other disciples done as Thomas did they would have sustained the same loss, and been the doubters.

The Scriptures nowhere hold out the idea that doubts are constitutional troubles, but the offspring of mistaken and sinful actions. Adam sinned and thereby lost confidence in God as a Father and Friend. There was no constitutional necessity for his distrust; he had never experienced it before. He did wrong, and, as a consequence, his heart condemned him, and he could not believe that God would approve him. Hence his distrust and vain effort to conceal himself.

So far from encouraging the disciples to view their unbelief as a constitutional defect, the Saviour positively taught them to regard it as a result of their own self-seeking and neglect of duty. "How can ye believe," said he, "which receive honor one of another, and seek not the

honor that cometh from God only?" Here unbelief is recognized as a necessity, and faith an impossibility, not because of constitutional difficulties, but because the love
of applause was indulged, and self-seeking had a place
in their actions. Such indulgence and actions they knew
to be improper, and by them they brought upon themselves self-reproach and raised an insuperable barrier to
confidence in God. On the other hand, this passage clearly
teaches that if we seek the honor that comes from God
only, or if, in utter self-abnegation, we accept all the will
of God, and hold our lives and our dearest rights subservient to his glory, we then can believe, whatever may be
the peculiarities of our mental constitution. We then have
"confidence toward God."

There is much other scripture teaching that feebleness
of faith and failures through unbelief depend, not upon
constitutional difficulties, but upon some want of conformity to the divine requirements and failure to observe
the conditions upon which strong and vigorous faith depends. Hence the Saviour said to his disciples who had
failed to cast out a demon, "This kind can come forth by
nothing but prayer and fasting; thus teaching them that
their failure was their fault, and that strong faith depended
upon matters under their control.

These truths of revelation are confirmed by the facts of
experience and observation. It is a fact that the doubters
of our own day are persons who are not careful to keep a
conscience void of offense. They read almost any thing
that comes to hand, talk on almost any subject, associate
with almost any kind of company, are careless about
closet and other devotions, and are not regarded by their
acquaintances as devoted persons. On the other hand, it
is a fact that men and women of strong faith are careful
about all these things; what they read, what they say,
what they do, what company they keep, and of every
thing else. They are close students of the Bible; much of

their time they live alone with God; and they keep on amicable terms with their own conscience and final Judge. This is the secret of their faith. They so live and act that their hearts do not condemn them, and, hence, have confidence toward God.

Notice, lastly, that the text makes the happy disclosure that,

5. *Confidence in God depends on natural and common sense principles.* — The same natural and common sense principles which underlie our confidence in man inspire confidence in God. If we wish our fellows to love and esteem us, and we to have the assurance of the fact, we keep on good terms with them. So we must keep on good terms with our Maker if we would feel assured that he loves and approves us. In our intercourse of man with man we cannot believe that a fellow will love and approbate us while we are mistreating him, and we are assured that he has knowledge of our course. Neither can we look to God and believe he loves and approves us while we are doing what we believe we should not do. This would imply a conviction that God is indifferent to our acts, and that he will indorse in us what we cannot indorse in ourselves. To try, therefore, to believe that God does approve and bless us, while our hearts condemn us, is to try to believe that God will approve vices in us which we ourselves disapprove. This must be an awful insult to God and a fearful slander upon his character.

I cannot go with confidence to a fellow for temporal assistance if I am compelled in truth to tell him that I am lazy and disinclined to work, and that what I do l execute carelessly. With such confessions I could not hope to get sympathy and help. But could I go and truthfully say that I had done all I could, and appeal to the benefactor for the truth of what I claimed, I should confidently expect a favorable hearing. Apply this principle to our approaches to God and the necessity of heart approval will appear. If we go to God and say, O Lord, we are doing the things we ought not to do, and leaving undone the things we ought to do; we are not worthy to take thy holy name upon our polluted lips— and we might add, and we expect to continue as we are; nevertheless, have mercy upon us and bless us; how, under such circumstances, can we have "confidence toward God?" Impossible!

But suppose we go with the same confession and can truthfully say, and appeal to God for the honesty of our purpose, O Lord, we are resolved that the sins of the past shall, by thy help, never be repeated, that we will hereafter and forever abstain from all appearance of evil and devote ourselves and all we have to thy glory, confidence immediately springs up in the heart, and we feel that earth and heaven are coming together, and we are embosomed in the sympathies and clasped in the arms of the Infinite Father. Such is the order of God and the law of the mind.

In these statements and facts is disclosed the secret of those troubles which so many have concerning their spiritual status, and their wrestlings and struggling to reach a more satisfactory religious experience. They are trying to persuade themselves that God will connive at certain practices or habits or states the propriety of which they doubt, but which they wish to retain. They are asking God to indorse them when, in the secret of their hearts, they cannot indorse themselves. They are asking God to do for them what in the very nature of things he cannot do until they change their attitude toward him.

IX
A Purifying Hope

And every man that hath this hope in him purifieth himself even as he is pure. —I John 3, 3.

WHAT HOPE? BY A REFERENCE to the preceding context it will be seen that it is not a hope that we have reached a gracious state, but a hope of seeing Christ as he is, and being like him, based upon the consciousness that we are now the sons of God. Among the many suggestions of the text it is proposed to notice only two leading thoughts.

1. *True Christians seek purity.* — It will be noticed that the verb "purifieth" is in the present tense. It does not intimate what the believer has done, or what he will do, but what he is now doing. He may have purified himself in the past, and may continue to purify himself in the future, and certainly will if he prove faithful; but it is what he is doing now that indicates the existence of a true evangelical hope. A true hope leads to present action and effort. "He purifieth himself." He cannot have an evangelical hope who is not now purifying himself, but pro-

poses to do it at some future time. All men, with very few exceptions, however degraded, have that kind of hope which springs from a purpose of future reform. Many professors of religion have no better hope. They acknowledge that they are not doing as they ought, but they intend to mend their ways by and by, and upon that purpose they claim a Christian hope. This is "the hope of unjust men that perisheth." It is affirmed in the text that "every man who has the hope of a true Christian *"purifieth* himself." It is the business of the present.

But what is it to purify one's self? It can mean nothing less than a desire for purity. He who hopes to spend his life in mercantile pursuits must desire a qualification for that business. So he who hopes to see Christ as he is and be like him, he who hopes to live forever with the purified citizens of heaven, must desire the purity necessary for the enjoyment of such a state and such company. His soul must hunger and thirst for righteousness. His language is, "As the hart panteth after the water-brooks, so panteth my soul after thee, O God. My soul thirsteth for God, for the living God."

To voluntarily retain any impurity of the flesh or spirit, or indulge any sin in the life, is to forfeit the favor of God. "If I regard iniquity in my heart," says the Psalmist, "the Lord will not hear me." Every true Christian, therefore, must desire purity of life and heart.

To purify one's self must mean more than a desire for purity. "He purifieth" expresses the idea of *action and effort*. The earnest Christian examines himself like an inspector of flour or other articles of traffic; to determine the quality within he pierces through himself. He proves himself, or applies tests to himself like the alchemist applies nitric acid to gold to test its integrity. Instead of applying the gospel square and plummet to others, a very common error, he is busy with himself. "He purifieth himself."

This language can mean nothing less than that he turns away from all sin, inward and outward, and to the full extent of his light he keeps himself unspotted from the world. It is a fearful mistake, which has crept into many of the different churches of late, that Christians may indulge certain habits and practice little vices which disturb religious peace and bring condemnation upon the soul, and yet claim the possession of an evangelical hope. "Every man that has this hope in him purifieth himself."

This language not only indicates a turning away from all sin, but the use of such means as God has ordained for the purification of the soul. A true Christian uses all the means of grace. He presses into use all losses and reverses, all prosperity and success, all disappointment and suffering. Like the worldling who presses all events and occurrences into the service of bearing down or pushing up stocks as his interests may demand, so the true believer presses all providences into the great and primary business of his life, the purification of his nature, and the development of his Christian character.

The language indicates, moreover, that a state of purity is retained by constant activity. Purity is not something that may be obtained and locked up in the heart and called upon when we need it, like a commodity which can be stored away in ware-rooms, but it is the divine nature inworked into the substratum of the soul, and retained by constant fidelity, by constant watchfulness and trust, or by a continued yielding to God and receiving the Holy Ghost. It is a *holy life lived*.

Notice next that the true Christian accepts,

2. *Christ as his standard of purity.* — "He purifieth himself, even as he is pure." There are some false standards of purity which every true believer must shun if he would reach what is provided for him in the atonement. It is proper for every member of the Church to examine closely the Discipline, the Confession of Faith, and the creed books

of his Church, and defer to their teachings, but he must not make them his ultimate standard of appeal in matters of religious experience. They may place the standard too low. The only safe rule of faith and practice is the Bible. And all true Christians desire and labor to be Bible Christians.

Again, the professors of religion around us must not be taken as patterns. Their spirit and lives may be very defective, and though many valuable hints and helps may be derived from their lives, yet to take them as patterns is to compare ourselves among ourselves and measure ourselves by ourselves, which, says the apostle, is not wise. One of the most fatal blunders that church members are making to-day is patterning after the religionists around them. This has been one of their blunders in every age. The Pharisee in one of the Saviour's parables made this fatal mistake. He was evidently one of the best men of his times. He could truthfully say, "I am not as other men are, extortioners, unjust, adulterers, or even as this publican. I fast twice in the week, I give tithes of all I possess." No doubt an honest comparison of himself with others around him, even with the professedly pious of his times, placed him, so far as the eye could detect, far in advance of his fellows. This led him to feel safe and to compliment himself. But had he consulted the writings of Moses and the prophets, and inquired for the spirit which God asked for in his children, he would have discovered his defects and penitently sought with deep abasement the required grace.

Thousands upon thousands of professed Christians are committing the same mistake to-day, and are hoping all will be right with them beyond the grave, because they compare favorably with what they see in the lives and spirit of their brethren.

Another false standard which many raise is what they call "more religion." He who is contented to seek "more religion" raises for his standard himself with a little accession to his graces, or raises a standard a little in advance of his present self. If it be said that by "more religion" he means a great deal more than he now has, still, if he means less than the purity of Christ, he has raised a false standard.

The standard here raised and accepted by the true Christian is practicable. The Saviour's life, so far as the moral elements involved in it are concerned, was an exemplification of what the Gospel proposes to do for our humanity. It was not the sole purpose of the incarnation to suffer and die for man, but part of the mission was to present a divine pattern of holy living; to show what the atonement provided for the believer. The practicability of this standard of purity, and imitability of this divine pattern, was exhibited in the religious life and triumphant death of the proto-martyr Stephen. His perfect devotion to the cause of Christ, and the complete imitation of the spirit of the Master in his death, "kneeling down and crying with a loud voice, Lord, lay not this sin to their charge," meaning his bloody murderers, shows the imitability of this pattern by fallen men through the power of grace. Hence, no earnest Christian who has come to see his privilege in the Gospel can aspire to less than what the atonement provides for him, nor can he feel satisfied with a standard of purity below that raised in the text. He will be restless until he has learned to live through faith like his divine Pattern, and with perfect purity of affections, of motives, of words, and of actions, he is assured of transparency of character. He must feel assured that, examined in the sunlight of eternity, no impurity will appear in his spirit, that it is washed and made "whiter than snow," and that he is "unblamable in holiness," and "unreprovable in his sight." "He purifieth himself even as he is pure."

X
BELIEVING AND CONFESSING

With the heart man believeth unto righteousness, and with the mouth confession is made unto salvation. — Romans 10. 10.

THE NECESSITY OF BELIEVING unto righteousness is conceded by all orthodox Christians, but confession unto salvation is viewed by many as an unimportant matter, and by others as a matter which it is more creditable for believers to omit. The inspired statement of the text, however, makes both exercises vital, and confession as necessary to salvation as believing is to righteousness. Examine

1. *Believing unto righteousness.*— 1.) The righteousness of which the apostle speaks he denominates "the righteousness of God," or "the righteousness of faith," to distinguish it from ceremonial righteousness. He means by it an inward state consisting of spiritual life, purity, and whatever else may be comprehended in being a partaker of the divine nature. He means, also, an outer life harmonizing with the word of God and exhibiting the graces of

love, peace, joy, long-suffering, gentleness, goodness, and other fruits of the Spirit. This state of the heart and manner of life, the apostle says, are produced by the Spirit through the belief of the heart. They are not the products of culture, discipline, and training, but of the Holy Ghost.

2.) The believing mentioned is not feeling or knowing, but the mind assenting to the truths, or at least the cardinal truths, of the Christian system. This assent is produced by the evidence which this system affords, external, internal and collateral, but chiefly by man's own spiritual intuitions of need and the source of supply. This consciousness of need and conviction of an adequate and available supply in Christ may lead to the renunciation of sin and acceptance of Him as a personal Saviour. And when this is the outcome of the mind's assent to the truth the person is said to believe with the heart unto righteousness.

3.) By the word "heart" the apostle means, as do all the inspired writers, the whole spiritual man. The Scriptures make no division of the mind into intellect, sensibilities and will, or any other psychological distribution of faculties. With the sacred writers the heart perceives, reflects, reasons and performs all other acts of the intellect; it loves, hates, enjoys, suffers, and performs all other functions of the sensibilities; and it wills, determines, plans and executes, and fills the offices of the will. Hence, to believe with the heart engages and calls into exercise the entire spiritual department of man's nature. It is such an assent of the mind to the truth, such a consent of the affections to the truth and such an acceptance of the truth by the will as places the soul in the hands of Christ to forgive, to heal, and to keep unto eternal life.

Special emphasis must be placed upon the word *believeth*, so as to distinguish it from *imagining* or *conjecturing*, from feeling, or trying to feel, and from knowing, or trying to know. The Spirit imparts righteousness through the heart's belief of God's record concerning his Son, and not through feeling, or knowledge, or the witness of the Spirit. Knowledge of the fact, the witness of the Spirit to the fact, and a joyful sense of the fact, must, in the nature of things, follow after the fact of deliverance takes place in the soul, and the fact of deliverance cannot take place till the heart believeth unto righteousness. Such is God's order. Notice.

2. *Confessing unto salvation.*— 1.) By *salvation* the apostle means more than righteousness. The belief of the heart is followed by righteousness, or a new heart and life, but it requires a confession of these facts with the mouth to reach what he calls salvation. There are many in the Church who have abandoned a sinful life and received Christ; they believe in him with the heart and are righteous; they are among the best and most reliable members of Christ's visible body, and yet they are not delivered from an enervating timidity and an enfeebling diffidence which interferes with their comfort and usefulness. They are not fully saved from self, from a man-pleasing and a man-fearing spirit, and from doubts as to their true inward state. They do not *enjoy their righteousness*; they have not *confessed unto salvation*.

Such is the divine arrangement that whoever would swing entirely free in associations and labors with Christians, and exert the influence and power among men which the Gospel offers, must confess Christ in the most open, definite, and pronounced manner. There must not only be a heartfelt, but also an *avowed* identification with the cause of Christ.

2.) There must be a confession with the mouth. Christian teachers and theologians may philosophize as much as they please upon the beauty, force and eloquent utterances of a holy life, and, indeed, too much cannot be said on the importance of such a life in order to meet the divine requirements and give credibility to testimony; yet *confession with the mouth* will ever be a necessity while the Holy Ghost continues to utter the language of the text. No living, however exemplary and holy, will answer as a substitute for confession with the mouth; nor will confession with the mouth answer as a substitute for holy living. Both are required.

The necessity for this vocal confession is laid in the constitution of human nature. Every one knows that any passion of the soul when excited is sensibly intensified by any utterance upon the exciting subject. Hence thoughtful persons, under the power of, or temptation to, anger, keep their mouths closed and turn from the temptation. They know that to open the mouth upon the exciting theme is to fire a magazine of powder. Hence also the necessity of frequent declarations of confidence and love between the members of the same household, and especially between those who are wedded for life. Accordingly every earnest Christian has noticed that distinct confessions of deadness to sin and life in God have greatly cleared and intensified his experience in these things. He has also noticed that the failure to confess with the mouth on proper occasions has been succeeded by more or less doubt and spiritual feebleness. And all who have indulged a protracted failure at this point have experienced conscious and painful loss of a happy union with the adorable Bridegroom.

3.) This confession of the mouth is to be as continuous as the believing with the heart. It is thought by some that when a confession of any gracious state, especially the state of entire sanctification, is made at any place there is no necessity, but rather an impropriety, in naming the matter in that place at any subsequent time; that any restatement of the fact only tends to spiritual pride and to awaken distrust and aversion in the minds of those who hear. But, while there are some who dislike to hear such statements repeated because it rebukes their lukewarmness, there are others who long to hear them again and again because of the encouragement it affords to them.

Besides, these two exercises, like the Siamese twins who were born and raised together, were joined in the divine conception of man's need, and must never be separated. A separation destroys both. A confession without righteousness is too hard to practice long, and righteousness without confession will soon smother to death. No matter, then, how much some spiritual guides of the people may extol silence concerning religious states, there can be no true and deep experience in divine things without declaring it with the mouth frequently, explicitly, and upon all proper occasions, not in any one set phrase, like a parrot, but in the beautifully diversified formulas of inspired language. The sainted Fletcher, and many others since his day, have tried to separate these exercises, but with sad results upon their experience.

Whoever, therefore, would have a clear and satisfactory religious experience; whoever would feel free in his religious exercises; whoever would reach the maximum of his spiritual power, and whoever would perpetuate these desirable experiences, must be, and continue to be, pronounced in his religious posture; he must burn all the bridges as he proceeds and leave no temptation to retreat; he must confess, and continue to confess, *with the mouth*, no matter what may be the mortifications of self and the pain it inflicts upon formalists and others at variance with God's order.

XI
CHRIST OUR SANCTIFICATION

> But of him are ye in Christ Jesus, who of God is made
> unto us wisdom, and righteousness, and sanctifica-
> tion, and redemption. —I Cor. 1. 30.

I T WILL BE NOTICED in the Authorized Version that
the principal words in this passage are separated
by commas, and are thereby made co-ordinate
words in the sentence. The Revised Version omits
one comma, and thus makes righteousness and
sanctification united co-ordinate with the remaining principal words. But the Greek of Scholz reads
righteousness, sanctification, and redemption, without commas, and makes these three words taken together co-ordinate and synonymous with wisdom.
This is most likely the correct punctuation, and gives
the reading, "Of him are ye in Christ Jesus, who is
made unto us wisdom from God, *even* righteousness
and sanctification and redemption." With this reading, which does not change the spiritual import of the
passage, but makes clear St. Paul's meaning of the
word wisdom, there are a few points to be noticed.

1. *A truly gracious state is "of him," and "in Christ Jesus."* — It is such a vital union with Christ, produced by the Holy Spirit, as Paul symbolized by wild olive grafted to the tame. This means a complete separation from the old trunk and a careful insertion into the new. As grafts must be cut from the parent tree to be inserted into another, so sinners must "come out from among them and be separate, and touch not the unclean thing," if they would be sons and daughters of the Almighty. And as grafts will not grow unless carefully pared by the grafter, and carefully set in so that bark fits to bark, and fiber to fiber, so sinners must submit to such surgery as may be necessary to fit them into the Christ nature. As not one of the many grafts that might be thrown loosely among the branches of the most healthy tree will grow unless carefully inserted by the husbandman, so not one of all the many who attend our Sunday-school and ordinances of religion will come into living union with Jesus, unless, becoming passive in the divine hand, the Holy Spirit prepare the heart and make the mystic insertion.

2. *When this union takes place Christ becomes to the believer wisdom from God.* — To understand the force of this expression it must be remembered that the facts and incidents of New Testament history transpired in what is called the Augustan Age. At the time of the apostle's writing the schoolmen and general populace of Corinth spent their time much as Luke says the Athenians and strangers did at Athens, "in nothing else, but either to tell or to hear some new thing." This desire of the popular mind for certain forms of knowledge and information led to the neglect of more important matters. Hence we read somewhere that long before Paul's day Demosthenes rebuked his countrymen for lounging about the market-places, with their everlasting inquiry for the news, instead of preparing for the attack of Philip of Macedon. But when any of these restless souls received Christ this de-

sire was properly tempered, and Christ became a satisfying portion. In him they found all the treasures of wisdom and knowledge. So, to-day, we live in the most enlightened period of the world's history. Thousands of books
are issued yearly by the secular and religious presses,
thousands upon thousands of monthlies and weeklies are
circulated through the country, and millions upon millions of dailies are scattered along the great highways of
travel, and there is an unhealthy longing for the news
that excludes the Bible and good books from the general
reading. But when these intemperate lovers of news receive Christ as a personal Saviour, and come into blessed
union and fellowship with him, whether they be preachers or laymen, he becomes to them wisdom from God,
and the restless search for information on secular matters gives way to the study of Jesus and his word.

3. *This wisdom from God consists in righteousness and
sanctification and redemption.* — By righteousness is
meant the fulfilling of that divine law under which man
was placed, requiring purity of heart and rectitude of life.
But because of the exceeding breadth of this law and the
disability which the fall entailed upon man he alone cannot possibly fulfill it. To meet this emergency Christ became man's substitute, and provided for his complete
deliverance from all the consequences of the fall. Thus
Christ becomes "the end of the law for righteousness to
every one that believeth." The perfect justification and
perfect salvation which perfect obedience to the law would
secure become possible now to the Christian through faith
in the Crucified. Thus he is made unto us righteousness,
and though the believer expects to be rewarded according to his works, he never looks to these for salvation, but
to the Lord Jesus by faith, *and faith only*.

Another element in this wisdom is sanctification, or
inward purity. There is a notion current that the purity of
the believer is Christ's purity simply imputed, and not

imparted; and that no inward work of purification is wrought in the heart of the believer this side of the dying hour. But the grafting symbol of the apostle compels the idea of imparted life, imparted purity, and imparted power. As the trunk imparts its life and fruitfulness to the graft, so Christ imparts his life and purity to the believer, and thus he becomes a partaker of the divine nature. Hence the Old Testament promise, "I will sprinkle clean water upon *you*, and *ye shall be clean*; from *all your filthiness*, and all *your idols will I cleanse you*." Hence also the New Testament promise, "the blood of Jesus Christ his Son *cleanseth us* from all sin." "If we confess our sins, he is just and faithful to forgive us our sins, and to *cleanse us* from all unrighteousness." Thus Christ becomes our sanctification by his indwelling Spirit; by coming into us, expelling every thing unlike himself, and living out his own pure life in us.

There is one more thing included in this wisdom from God, denominated by the apostle, redemption. This word generally comprehends the whole work of salvation, from the pardon of sin to the soul's eternal deliverance; but here its meaning seems to be confined to the soul's glorification, though apprehended as a present realization. Said an eminent divine recently, "Christ has become my righteousness and sanctification, and I expect him by and by to become my redemption." This, however, is not the tense used by the apostle, nor does it convey his meaning. He used a past tense in the Greek, and it is rendered in the Revised Version, "*was made* unto us redemption." The faith that truly apprehends Christ as our righteousness and sanctification "is the substance of things hoped for, the evidence of things not seen," and apprehends redemption as a present fact, though in promise. It is the equivalent of the Saviour's statement, "He that believeth on me hath everlasting life." He *hath*, not will have, life, the nature of which is to last forever, if not destroyed. So

Christ has become redemption, eternal deliverance to the true believer, and ever will be, during the continuance of this vital union.

4. *Whatever gift or grace the believer may see provided in the atonement and offered to him in the Gospel must be sought in the Christ already received.* — He must not go abroad in quest of the favor. "The word is nigh thee, even in thy mouth, and in thy heart." Whatever real want the believer may have arises from a failure to scripturally appropriate Christ; and a continual and proper appropriation of him will be a continual supply to Christian life, will furnish all necessary religious wisdom and impart complete spiritual purity and power. "Christ is all, and in all."

XII
THE SPIRIT OF TRUTH

Howbeit when he, the Spirit of truth, is come, he will guide you into all truth; for he shall not speak of himself; but whatsoever he shall hear, that shall he speak; and he will show you things to come. —John 16. 13.

THE ADVERB "WHEN" in the text refers to the Pentecost. "The Spirit " mentioned was the Holy Spirit who was to come at the Pentecost, inaugurate his reign, and establish himself in the New Testament Church forever. He was called "the Spirit of truth" because he first made known the truths of revelation to the prophets, the apostles, and other inspired teachers, and because he is to continue the expounder of these truths throughout all the ages. Hence he is here promised as the Teacher and Guide of all who believe. It is proposed now to examine a few of the salient points of this passage.

1. *The truth mentioned.*— The Authorized Version seems to use the word truth in a general sense, as though all kinds of truth were intended, but the Greek text uses

the definite article before it, limiting the meaning to a particular kind of truth. And no doubt the Saviour intended the word as here used to be confined wholly to revealed or spiritual truth, and to exclude all historic, philosophic, and scientific truth. Some one has very happily said that the Holy Spirit in his illuminating office is to the soul what the head-light is to the railway locomotive. As it sheds its light directly on the track, showing the rails, the culverts, the bridges, and whatever obstructions may have come upon the road, and incidentally sheds a few scattering rays upon the adjacent fields and forests through which it passes, so the Holy Spirit casts his radiance directly upon the path of life, revealing it and all that imperils the traveler or impedes spiritual progress; but it is merely incidental that any light is shed upon cognate themes. Hence the Greek text, literally rendered, reads, The Spirit of *the* truth will guide you into all *the* truth," showing that the Spirit's enlightening office has sole reference to spiritual things.

2. *The guidance into all truth.* — It is not to be understood by this promise that all believers will be guided into all spiritual truth, but into so much of it as each may need for his personal salvation and personal work. It will be readily seen that the child will not need so much as the adult, the layman so much as the clergyman, and the greater the responsibilities the greater the measure of the divine illumination needed. And it is reasonable and scriptural to suppose that each believer in right moral relations with God would receive all needed light, and no more than he can properly use and make conducive to the glory of God. The Divine Being makes no investments which he does not intend to be remunerative.

Again, all needed light is not flashed at once upon the mind and heart by the Spirit, but gradually, through prayerful study and meditation, and then only as the light received is practiced. The Saviour said, "Take my yoke upon you, and learn of me." Here the order to learn implies thought and study; and the thought and study, to be effective in this department of knowledge, must be preceded by a submission to God and an acceptance of the yoke of Christ. "The secret of the Lord is with them that fear him," and with none others. No one can discern the mind of God in the Scriptures by any amount of study intended to merely increase his knowledge, or intended for the higher purpose of merely instructing others, without personal practice and obedience. Mere theorists are miserably poor teachers of divine things.

3. *The manner of this guidance.* — In different ages of the Church many have perverted this, and other promises of the Spirit's leading, to their great injury. They have supposed that to follow the Spirit it is only necessary to yield to internal promptings, without any study of Providence or Scripture or other sources of information, and have been thereby led into various forms of error and folly. Hence it is vital to know how the Spirit proposes to guide believers; and to find this mode it is only necessary to pay attention to scriptural teachings upon this subject. Notice the statements in the text, "For he shall not speak of himself; but whatsoever he shall hear, that shall he speak." The *apo* rendered "of" should be rendered *from,* and is so rendered in the Revised Version, and conveys the idea that the Holy Spirit will not manufacture or originate any new truth, but will simply transmit or impart that which he receives from the Father and the Son. Notice also in connection with this one of the last statements of revealed truth: "If any man shall add unto these things, God shall add unto him the plagues that are written in this book: and if any man shall take away from the words of the book of his prophecy, God shall take away his part out of the book of life." Hence all the impressions which come from the Holy Spirit, all the pointings of providence that ought to be followed, all the counsels of others that

ought to be heeded, and all the instruction from other sources that ought to be taken, will harmonize with the Bible; and to the teachings of this book all impressions, notions, counsels, etc., must be brought and tested.

By noticing, moreover, the manner by which the sacred characters of the Old and New Testament determined the mind of the Spirit and shaped their course, great light is shed upon the mode of the Spirit's leadings. Take as a sample, for the purpose of aiding the reader in tracing this matter as far as he may choose, the manner in which Paul shaped his treatment of others. Now let it be remembered that Paul enjoyed the guidance of the Spirit as tendered in the promises of the New Testament, and yet he says, "Unto the Jews I became as a Jew, that I might gain the Jews; to them that are under the law, as under the law, that I might gain them that are under the law; to them that are without law, as without law, that I might gain them that are without law. To the weak became I as weak, that I might gain the weak; I am made all things to all, that I might by all means save some. And this I do for the gospel's sake." It is clear from this that Paul, to find out the course the Spirit would have him take in the work of saving others, exercised his common sense, deferred as far as possible, not to compromise the great principles of the Gospel, to the notions, prejudices, and opinions of those whom he would save, and followed in all cases good sanctified common sense. Similar lessons are deducible from the manner these characters determined their course in other matters.

4. *The things to come which the Spirit will show.* — The literal rendering is, he will announce to you things coming; indicating some revealings of the future more or less remote, and which natural reason cannot foresee. The original promise may have had special allusion to the prophecies uttered by the apostles after the ascension of their Lord and the descent of the Holy Ghost, but it must

be allowed a wider application. For it is a fact to-day that many who live near the Lord have disclosures of the future made to them of which mere nominal Christians know nothing. A pious parent pleads for the awakening and conversion of a recreant child and receives an assurance that the event will take place. A sanctified wife prays for her husband afflicted with a mortal malady which no medical remedies can reach, and is answered by an inward conviction, which she knows to be divine and exclusive of all doubt, that he shall survive. An anointed soul-saver asks the Lord, as he enters upon special services for this purpose, for one, five, or ten hundred conversions, and he announces at the opening of his labors the number promised. And these several events happen according to the faith that claimed them, and which was honored by the Holy Spirit in revealing them beforehand to the suppliants. And much more of these revealings would be vouchsafed to believers did they live nearer to God, and honor more by their faith the blessed Revealer of things to come.

But there is another sense in which the Holy Spirit will show believers, in whose hearts he dwells as the Comforter, things to come. He gives substantiality to the eschatological subjects of revelation. To the average Christian of this day the resurrection of the body, the day of final judgment, and the future state of rewards and punishments are wrapped in the dreamy mysticism of speculation and doubt. The Holy Spirit, when received in his fullness, dissipates this mist, and brings these subjects from the sphere of the mythical into the real, and thereby shows things to come, and becomes the Conservator of the great truths of revelation.

XIII
TWO PHASES OF CHRISTIAN EXPERIENCE

Let us lay aside every weight and the sin which doth so easily beset us and let us run with patience the race that is set before us. —Heb. 12. 1.

THIS LANGUAGE IS ADDRESSED to believers who have entered the Christian race and are pressing toward the prize. The apostle modestly tells them that they are running at a disadvantage, and might progress with more satisfaction to themselves and with greater certainty as to final results. In this exhortation two distinct phases of spiritual life are clearly brought to view, and are distinguished by marked characteristics. They are distinguished,

1. *By weights.* — One carries weights, the other is free from them. It is a matter of universal experience, and a fact obvious to every careful observer, that the common religious life is hindered by family cares, business troubles, and neighborhood difficulties. These are allowed to interfere with closet devotions, family prayers, and church duties. Feebleness of faith, and a hidden defect in

consecration, separate between religious and secular duties, and array them frequently against each other, so that legitimate cares and imperative duties often become weights sensibly felt in the Christian race.

The apostle orders a change in this matter. "Let us lay aside every weight." He does not order the abandonment of business and attention to family interests, but to so fully consecrate self, family, business, and all other interests to God that attention to secularities is as much a religious work as closet and family prayer. They will then never conflict. Each class of duties will then receive its appropriate share of attention; and since all is done to the glory of God there will be no painful solicitude as to the success or failure of plans and measures. These and all other matters are committed to God, and the soul is at rest. As the traveler upon entering the car no longer carries his satchel, but places it at his feet and guards it, merely, so the believer, in entering upon this higher plane of religious life, casts all his cares upon him who careth for him, and guards them there, that no man take his crown.

These phases of spiritual life are distinguished again by—

2. *The besetting sin.*— The apostle, it will be observed, uses the singular noun *sin*, and not *sins* in the plural. Believers are not troubled with *sins*. They have abandoned all sins or sinful acts. Hence, "Whosoever abideth in him sinneth not," and "Whosoever is born of God doth not commit sin." Whoever, therefore, habitually indulges in sinful acts of any kind— that is, known sinful acts— whether he belongs to the Church or not, is an unrepentant sinner. He may not be as sinful as some other grade of sinners, nevertheless he moves in the same downward course and will reach the same dreadful future. The apostle makes no reference here to actual sins, but what he calls in other places "the sin that dwelleth in me." This principle of evil in us is a unit, and lies back of and produces all

actual sin, and may well be styled "*the sin* that doth so easily beset." In the Christian not freed from its inbeing it is ever rising, and trying to break through his weak points into actual sins. Hence many Christians have trouble with their temper, many with their pride, many with coveteousness, many with other forms of sin, and all with more or less unbelief.

Now the apostle orders his brethren, and through them all imperfect believers, to lay aside this inherent bias to evil, so that it will no longer trouble them, nor interfere with their religious progress. He does not order the repression of this bias, but, Áðïôéèçìé, to put away from, to lay aside never to be taken up again. He, moreover, uses the aorist tense of this verb, or the aorist participle, indicating a finished action — done once for all, and never to be repeated. It is clear, therefore, from this scripture that there is a form of religious life which is free from the besetting sin, and must be free from every other. Christian watchfulness in such a life is not directed to the repression of evil tendencies, but to guarding against the entrance of evil into the purified heart.

Another distinguishing mark of these two forms of spiritual life is found in —

3. *The religious movements.* — Having "laid aside every weight, and the sin which doth so easily beset," the believer is ready to run with patience the race which is set before him. This supposes a tardy and impatient movement until all obstacles are removed. And it is a matter of fact that in the lower planes of religious life there is a slow growth, and more or less impatience felt, if not exhibited, in church work and in the endurance of the various religious trials. The state of the soul in this experience and the character of its devotions are well expressed in the favorite hymn of such worshipers:

"Look how we grovel here below,
  Fond of these earthly toys;
Our souls, how heavily they go,
  To reach eternal joys."

The higher experience drops this doleful strain and takes up one of more cheer and life. There is a fullness of spiritual life as there is of animal or physical life. There are many persons whose vital forces are so low that they move with slow and measured tread, while there are others so full of vitality that they cannot be quiet. Their movements are almost constant, and often violent; and they not unfrequently, from sheer plethora of vital force, annoy their more quiet neighbors. Thus there are a few whose spiritual life is so plethoric that they are restless in their rest, and violent in their tranquillity, and disturb the peace of their less active brethren. Their movements seem so hurried, so earnest, so radical, that those who sing Watts's hymn, from which the quotation above has just been made, do not understand them. Those only can appreciate their movements and understand their zeal who have felt the same mighty impulses of a purified nature, and worship with the triumphant song of prevailing Israel:
  "Lame as I am, I take the prey!
    Hell, earth, and sin with ease o'ercome;
  I leap for joy, pursue my way,
    And as a bounding hart fly home."

Surely no one, not biased by a theory, but open to conviction, can fail to see in this scripture two well-marked phases of religious life. Nor can he fail to see that the higher plane is not reached by the gradual progress of development, but by a definite and specific act of renunciation, consecration, and faith. The laying aside of every weight, and the sin that doth so easily beset, indicate, by the aorist tense already noticed, a well-marked emergence from a burdened and restrained spiritual life to one unburdened and free; from a tardy and impatient religious state to one of speed and serenity, and from one not wholly satisfactory to one completely meeting all the complex demands of the soul.

In the next verse the apostle gives us to understand that this high order can only be executed, and the grand results of its execution be realized, by a constant looking unto Jesus. The acts of renunciation and consecration by which, through divine help, the higher Christian experience is reached, are momentary, and finished once for all; but the acts by which this state of rest and life of victory are perpetuated, are continuous, and must not cease until the purified believer shall be summoned to the sunnier heights of the celestial land.

XIV
SPIRITUAL HUNGER AND THIRST

Blessed are they which do hunger and thirst after righteousness: for they shall be filled. —Matt. 5. 6.

THE RIGHTEOUSNESS SPOKEN OF here being something which the soul may hunger for and take in, it means a correct inward state, or purity of the heart. It is "Christ in you the hope of glory," imparting and preserving the divine nature in believers. Of course this inward righteousness will manifest itself in a correct outward life, but the inward state is the primary thought here.

1. As food for the body is elaborated in the vegetable systems and animal organisms outside and independent of the body itself, so the righteousness for which the soul should hunger and thirst is something extrinsic to it and must come from abroad. As no amount of exercise can produce food in the system to develop its functions, so no amount of culture and discipline can awaken spiritual life in the soul or develop pure desires and holy dispositions. Christ, "who is our life," must be taken into the heart. "Except ye eat the flesh

of the Son of man, and drink his blood, ye have no life in you."

As there are artificial flowers which look like the natural rose and lily but emit not the fragrance of the living blossoms, and as there are wax figures which look as though they could move and speak but have no animal organism and life, so there are persons born in Christian families, educated in Christian schools, and disciplined in Christian Churches, who appear much like Christians, and may be mistaken for them, but they have no spiritual life, cannot speak the language of Canaan, and can do no spiritual work. Spiritual life is an exotic, and must be transplanted in the soul from a foreign clime.

2. For the bread and water of life the soul must hunger and thirst, but these appetites imply antecedent life. We never predicate hunger and thirst of inorganic matter. True, we say poetically, The thirsty earth drinks the falling rain, but in this connection we use the word tropically, and in a very different sense from what we use it when we say, The thirsty ox drinks from the flowing brook. To hunger and thirst after righteousness, therefore, implies antecedent spiritual life. The penitent sinner cannot properly be said, as is often done, to hunger and thirst after righteousness. He longs to be free from guilt and misery, and if this longing may be called hunger and thirst, it cannot be said to be after righteousness, or likeness to God. Only truly regenerated persons, walking abreast of their light, and yearning for the divine nature, truly hunger and thirst after righteousness. Much of what is called hungering and thirsting after righteousness by church members is nothing more than a yearning to get clear of condemnation contracted by careless living. They are far from longing to be dead to self, to go to crucifixion, to love as Christ loved, and to lay down their life for the brethren. This is the divine righteousness spoken of by the Saviour.

Again, hunger not only implies life, but life ordinarily in good condition. Stout and hearty persons go readily to the table at suitable times and take their food with avidity and pleasure. So they are the most spiritual members of the Church who are the most ready to bow at an altar of prayer, or engage in any exercise that promises strength to the heart. And as a want of physical hunger at suitable times indicates a diseased condition of the body, and a protracted want of appetite for food is alarming, and calls for medical attention, so a want of spiritual hunger at suitable times declares a diseased condition of the soul, and a continued absence of this appetite indicates a state spiritual death. The animal that never hungers nor eats is dead; so church-members who never long for nor take spiritual food are dead, and utterly insensible to their condition.

3. The Saviour speaks of thirst in connection with hunger, and must mean something by it. Hunger is for the solids of nourishment and thirst for the liquids. The liquids, though wholly or partly innutritious, nevertheless serve an important and necessary part in the animal economy. They form a lubricating material for the joints, and give flexibility to the muscular parts of the frame. Now righteousness has its solids for which the soul should hunger. They are the unbending principles of justice, rectitude, and holiness. It has also its liquids for which the soul should thirst. They are mercy, long-suffering, gentleness, goodness, and the like, which give suitable flexibility to the sterner principles just named. There are certain characters among good people who are so unbendingly just and unswervingly honest that they wear an exactness and severity which make them disagreeable company to milder natures. They need the liquids of righteousness. Then there are certain others to be met with who are so flexible as to be unreliable. There seems to be no

bone in their religious character. They need the solids of righteousness.

It was not a mere accident that the Saviour spoke of thirsting in connection with hungering, and that he said on another occasion, "Except ye eat the flesh of the Son of man, and drink his blood, ye have no life in you." Whatever may be the Saviour's meaning in "hunger and thirst," and "eat the flesh and drink the blood," they must not be interpreted to mean less than receiving all the Christ-nature and life; its rectitude and holiness, as well as its gentleness and love.

4. Hunger and thirst for righteousness is here viewed as a volitional state of the heart, and hence rewardable. Physical hunger is more or less under the control of the will. When persons find their bodily appetite for food insufficient they change the atmosphere about them, stir themselves to greater activity, change the character of their diet, and, if necessary, take a tonic of some kind. So members of the Church who discover a want of spiritual appetite should change the religious atmosphere around them by changing their company and books; they should stir themselves to greater activity in the use and means of grace and in Christian work; and make such confessions to the brethren as will place them in their right attitude before the Church, and such consecrations as will put them in right moral relations with God.

5. The Saviour affirms of those who have this hungering and thirsting that they are blessed, or happy. He says in the same connection, "blessed are they that mourn," "blessed are the poor in spirit," "blessed are they which are persecuted for righteousness' sake," and so on. Now poverty of spirit, the spirit of mourning, the feeling of hunger and thirst, persecution and reviling, are not pleasant, and productive of happy emotions, yet the Saviour pronounces them happy who have these experiences. They are happy, because these experiences indicate right

conditions and right moral relations. Hence, the Saviour takes more account, as all ought to do, of right attitudes than of happy emotions.

6. The Saviour says of all who hunger and thirst, or are in a right condition, *"they shall be filled."* Nor does the future tense here refer to a distant period, but one very near at hand. Ordinarily the meals are ready as soon as the hunger commences. The seasons of hunger and meal time come together. So the believer may receive by faith the imperishable bread as soon as the hunger is sufficient. He ought not to look upon continuous hunger the highest gracious state, but hunger satisfied; as continuously recurring seasons of hunger and eating, thirsting, and drinking, so in healthy spiritual life there are continuously recurring seasons of hunger and thirst, of receiving and filling, and growing and maturing.

XV
FILLED WITH THE SPIRIT

"Be filled with the Spirit." —Eph. 5, 18.

YOU WILL NOTICE THAT the word spirit is spelled with a capital S, indicating that it is a proper noun, the name of a person. The reference is to that Divine Personage who proceeds from the Father and the Son, and called the Spirit of Christ, the Spirit of God, the Spirit of holiness, the Spirit of truth, but more generally known by the adorable title The Holy Ghost. The office of this Spirit is to convince the sinner of his guilt and danger, lead him to Christ, regenerate and adopt the penitent believer, to witness to that adoption, to lead him on to perfect holiness, to witness to that gracious state, to change the purified believer "into the same image from glory to glory as by the spirit of the Lord."

1. The text intimates that believers may possess different measures of the Spirit. The Holy Spirit as a creative and sustaining power fills saints and sinners alike. He fills all beings, and all things, and all spaces; for there is

no point in the universe where he is not, in all his attributes and perfections. But as a saving force he exists in different degrees or different measures in different persons, or in different degrees in the same person at different times or seasons. And this must not be interpreted to mean that the Spirit is a mere influence, and that we are speaking of different degrees of an influence. When we receive the Holy Spirit in any measure we receive him in the entirety of his personality; for he is indivisible. But because he is repressed by a stubborn or ignorant human will he reveals himself only in some of his offices. When, however, the believer lifts the repressive force of his will by a complete and irreversible self-surrender, giving the Spirit full right of way through the whole being, he reveals himself in all his offices, and all such believers are said to be filled with the Spirit. The sinner has the Spirit in his illuminating office, and when he surrenders to the Spirit he receives him in his regenerating and adopting offices, and if he follow on to know the Lord he will soon receive him in his purifying and empowering offices; or, in other words, he becomes filled with the Spirit, and executes the order of the text.

2. To be filled, therefore, with the Spirit is to be so emptied of self, and every thing earthly, and so occupied with salvation, personal and general, that divine things become the object of primary thought and attention. A politician is said to be filled with his subject when, start him on what theme you may, he will soon be on his favorite topic. He cannot help it. He is filled with the theme. Ask him to do this or that, or go here or there, or accept this or that measure, the question immediately arises, What will be the probable result of such measures on my political hopes? and he will accept nothing, nor do any thing, that may deplete the votes which he hopes to get. Like as this political aspirant bears insult from his constituents with great meekness rather than lose their suffrage, or

the covetous worldling gently enduring all manner of abuse from his customers rather than lose their patronage, so a Christian filled with the Spirit bears with meekness and long-suffering abuse and insult rather than imperil his religious hopes. All measures and enterprises must be clearly stamped by the divine signature or they are rejected, and all questions touching conduct must be solved in this way; and all this with pleasure and delight. David evidently referred to this state of the heart when he said of the blessed man of the first Psalm, "His delight is in the law of the Lord and in his law doth he meditate day and night."

3. The text assumes that all Christians may be filled with the Spirit. The characters originally addressed were not very promising church members, according to the popular notions of hopeful converts. The antecedents of many in the Church at Ephesus, as we learn from the general trend of the epistle, were not the most favorable to an after life of holiness and usefulness. There were among them converted drunkards, converted liars, converted thieves, and converted felons of various grades, and yet the apostle insists on them being filled with the Spirit. Indeed, the Greek verb is an imperative, present, passive, and would literally read, Continue to be filled with the Spirit; assuring this to be their state at the time, and ordering such a course as would preserve it. How empty therefore, the excuses generally given by church members for inattention to this great need of every believer! Nervous or lymphatic temperaments, high-strung nervous constitutions or the opposite, perplexing business relations, unfavorable family connections, and all other similar excuses are much less in the way of obtaining and retaining the fullness of the Spirit than the former habits of converted thieves, liars, and drunkards. All may be filled with the Spirit.

4. The text not only expresses a privilege, but enforces

a duty. It is imperative. God orders his people to be filled with the Spirit; and to attempt a compromise— by being and doing a little better than at present, or being and doing much better, if short of the fullness of the Spirit— is to grieve and disobey God. Yet thousands upon thousands of professing Christians fall into this terrible snare, supposing that being and doing *better* is the equivalent of being and doing *right*. The result of this is that the mass of church members never get beyond the experience of the "flesh lusting against the Spirit, and the Spirit against the flesh," and remain shamefully weak in their spiritual life, and inefficient in their work. To this want of the fullness of the Spirit is to be attributed the sad failures of many pulpits and pews. The perfunctory teaching of the Scriptures in many Sunday-schools, and the professional preaching by too many pulpits, for the last quarter of a century, have hardened the pupils and lowered the spirituality of many churches. "The letter killeth."

Our religious orators have waxed unusually eloquent as they have portrayed the magic power of the Sunday-school not only to replenish the Church as death depletes the membership, but also to rapidly swell the number of the saints on earth. While this is true in theory, and ought to be in realization, the fact is, the boys, in many places, before they reach their majority, leave the schools, wander off to resorts of pleasure, to places of vice, and are rarely ever seen about the churches. They were not brought into contact with "the Spirit that quickeneth," but with "the letter that killeth." Scarcely one in twenty of the young men who attended Sunday-schools in their boyhood, taking the country over, now belong to churches; and the case is little better with the young women. It is indecorous for them to promenade the streets on Sunday, to hide away and play cards, to go on Sunday excursions to watering-places and beer-gardens, and to spend the holy Sabbath in this manner; hence they go to church, and many become members. But too few really repent, truly receive Christ, and become true, spiritually-minded Christians. Many remain unconverted, dress as gaily as the young women of the world, enjoy its pleasures as well as other worldlings, and have no spiritual life. All this takes place because so many Sunday-school workers, class-leaders, and church officials remain destitute of the fullness of the Spirit, and "kill" those under their care. "Our sufficiency is of God; who also hath made us able ministers of the new testament; not of the letter, but of the spirit; for the letter killeth, but the spirit giveth life."

5. The text is an imperative, present, passive, in the Greek Scriptures, and if it does not mean the characters addressed were already filled, and urges them to a continuance in this state, it does assume that they were in right moral relations to receive this fullness. The order is not to get ready, or to take steps to be filled, but to take the fullness now, without any other step or preparatory work. Many believers reaching after this grace go over and over the preparatory work and make the fatal blunder of not taking the coveted blessing. They wait for something that can never take place; they wait for God to change his order, and let them feel and be assured of possession before they believe; thus leaving no place for faith, the divinely-appointed condition of salvation. God's order in grace is the same as in nature. First, the facts, then a belief of the facts, then feelings suitable to the facts believed, and then a course of action suitable to the facts, the beliefs, and the feelings. Our business is to meet the conditions upon which this fullness is promised, and then claim it, hit or miss, sink or swim, survive or perish, feeling or no feeling. Whoever will do this, and hold steadily to the position, shall as certainly be filled, and the fact made known to his consciousness, as that God exists. Glory to the Lamb!

XVI
ISHI, NOT BAALI

"And it shall be at that day, saith the Lord, that thou shall call me Ishi, and shall call me no more Baali." — Hos. 2. 16.

THERE ARE DEGREES in alienation from God. All sinners are far from him, but some are farther, and some are farthest. There are bad, worse, worst— among the unconverted. So, while all true Christians are near to God, some are nearer, and some are nearest. There are good, better, best among the pious. There are degrees in salvation, or stages in the religious life.

One of the most interesting methods by which inspiration represents the different degrees of affinity between God and his people is in the use of the amicable relations existing among men. Prominent among these, and embracing all others, are the servant, the child, and the spouse.

1. *The lowest plane upon which God's people may be found is that of mere servants.* — The religious life com-

mences upon this low plane, serving God for wages— to escape hell and gain heaven. The apostles commenced at this point, and hence Peter said: "We have left all and followed thee; what shall we have therefore? But before the Saviour left the world he had occasion to say to these disciples: "Henceforth I call you not servants, ...but friends"— intimating a nearer affinity than at the beginning of their religious life. This low plane, however, excludes all voluntary sinful action. "No man can serve two masters... Ye cannot serve God and mammon."

2. *A higher degree of affiliation is represented by the child-relation.*— Hence we read, "Wherefore thou art no more a servant, but a son." "And because ye are sons, God hath sent forth the Spirit of his Son into your hearts, crying, Abba, Father." Endearing as this relation is, it involves the notion of service, but on a much higher plane than that of a hireling. "The heir, as long as he is a child, differeth nothing from a servant, though he be lord of all." But children do not serve for the patrimony to be inherited, but because they love their parents and the family to which they belong. They are actuated by love, and from that motive they serve whether there be any property to descend or not.

So there is a gracious state in which the believer serves God and the Church, not to escape hell and gain heaven, though this first prompted the effort, but for the pleasure there is in the service. Love for God and the institutions of Christianity leads the thoughts and the activities.

As it happens that right-minded children sometimes feel a willfulness and an opposition to some of the parent's arrangements, so it happens that God's loving children sometimes feel an aversion to the heavenly Father's arrangements, which leads them to cry out,

"'Tis worse than death my God to love
And not my God alone."

To relieve his people of this native perversity God has provided for its removal and their elevation to a perfected union with himself, symbolized by the marriage relation. Hence notice,

3. *The highest affinity of God's people with himself is brought to view in the scripture heading this article,* — "Thou shalt call me Ishi" — my husband — "and shalt call me no more Baali" — my lord. The most intimate of all the amicable relations implies service, but with an affection which renders the most menial service a pleasure.

To live in wedded union with one loved more tenderly than any other on earth is the climax of terrestrial life, and is the state to which every human being in the normal condition of man aspires. In its embrace the wife gladly sinks her name into her husband's; merges her property into his; chooses his fortunes, whether good or bad, as her own; accepts his honor or disgrace, and, in short, becomes one and inseparable with her husband in all joys and sorrows, and all the possible successes and reverses of this life. So in this highest phase of Christian life the believer sinks his name with Christ. He becomes in the highest sense a Christian — an anointed one; his property becomes the practically acknowledged possession of Christ; his honor and reputation go up or down as his Lord's; he stands identified with his Saviour in effort to save the world; in short, he is one and inseparable with the Crucified One.

If each of the married pair abandons the personal habits that may be wrong, and takes on the other's habits that may be right, there will follow a continually increasing affection for each other, and a continuous assimilation to each other in affinities, choices, and mental peculiarities. Indeed, it is said the physiognomy or facial outlines of such a wedded pair assimilate to each other. So the completed union with Christ is not a finality, but rather the beginning of an unfettered and rapid assimilation to his likeness which is never to end.

It ought to be noted that the Scripture suggesting these thoughts reads, "Thou shalt call me Ishi." Hence, to reach this highest plane of service is imperative, and not an optional matter with the people of God, as too many seem to think. And this affectionate address cannot be used by believers in any lower stage of experience. Indeed, some believers complain of their brethren who have come into wedded union with their Lord that they seem irreverent, and address the Divine Majesty in terms too familiar. The secret is, they are married to him, and enjoy a communion with him unknown to all living in a lower experience.

These different relationships which God's people are represented as enjoying are real, and should no more be jumbled together and confounded in thought and act than the corresponding relations among men. What would be the state of society if the servant, the child, and the spouse, claimed the same rights and took the same liberties? And the confusion of these well-defined relationships in spiritual life, or a want of discrimination in the stages of Christian, experience, has made bad work in the Christian Church.

But while this language is imperative it is also a tender proposal. And all that is necessary for one in the conscious enjoyment of love for Jesus to consummate this blessed union is to accept the proposal, reckon it done, and declare the fact. It is a valid and legal marriage in some States when lovers declare before witnesses their purpose to live together as husband and wife. So it is a divinely legalized marriage with Jesus when the true evangelical believer, rejecting all rivals of the Saviour, accepts a wedded union with him, with all that is included in such union, believes or reckons that it takes place, and puts himself in this attitude before the Church and the world.

XVII
THE WITNESS OF THE SPIRIT

Ye know all things. —I John 2. 20.

T HE NOTION THAT the witness of the Spirit is confined to the gracious state of pardon and
adoption is surely both unreasonable and
unscriptural. That it should ever have obtained favor among the wise and scholarly of the Church is
certainly one striking proof of the liability of such
persons to fall into the most illogical conclusions
upon divine themes. It would seem a necessary inference, a conclusion which no rational mind could escape, that, if the Holy Spirit is to be a Teacher, a Guide,
and a Comforter to believers, if it is true that he will
guide us into all truth," and that "he shall teach us
all things" concerning salvation, and especially concerning personal holiness, he must make known, as a
necessary part of this work, every state and condition of the soul. Accordingly, it is in harmony with
Scripture and universal experience to assert that the
Spirit witnesseth to his own work in the human heart,
whatever that work may be.

1. When the Spirit sheds light upon the sinner's mind, and convinces him of his guilt and condemnation, he witnesseth to this so clearly that the awakened person *feels* and *knows* that he is a sinner, and so exposed to the second death. No logic can convince him to the contrary while this witness remains. Kind friends may try to persuade him he has always been good, and that there is no occasion for his distress of mind; but he knows better. He has a divine witness to his condition. He may not know that this experience is the work and witness of the Holy Spirit, but may suppose that it is the result of his own cognitions; nevertheless the fact of guilt and condemnation is an absolute certainty to him.

2. When this light is followed, and the awakened sinner abandons his sins and accepts Christ by penitence and faith, he is pardoned, regenerated, and adopted into the divine family. Guilt is removed, and condemnation is lifted from the heart, the power of sin is broken, peace flows into the soul, and the happy convert is persuaded of the divine favor. To this work of instituting new relations and imparting new life the Spirit bears clear witness. The new convert now *feels* and *knows* that a change has taken place, and that he is now in favor with God. He is now as certain of the divine favor as in the awakening he was certain of the divine displeasure. He has received the "Spirit of adoption, whereby we cry, Abba, Father."

3. Sooner or later after the work of regeneration the faithful convert discovers a residuum of the evil nature lingering in the heart and manifesting itself in the form of pride, envy, self-will, worldliness, or other forms of depraved disposition. The witness of the Spirit in the heart now is that, "The flesh lusteth against the Spirit, and the Spirit against the flesh; and these are contrary the one to the other; so that ye cannot do the things that ye would;"

and the believer *knows* and *feels*, as in the other cases, that the work of grace is not completed in his heart. He is as sure of remaining impurity as, at the time of his awakening, he was of guilt and condemnation, and no amount of sophistry can persuade him to the contrary so long as he does not grieve and turn away the Spirit. He has the "Spirit of adoption" crying, "As he which hath called you is holy, so be ye holy, in all manner of conversation; because it is written: Be ye holy, for I am holy." Thus the Spirit witnesseth to his work of conviction for holiness as distinctly as to the conviction for pardon.

4. When this new light is followed by the believer, and he "yields himself unto God, as those that are alive from the dead," accepting Jesus as his sanctification, the work of entire purification is wrought, and the Spirit witnesses to it as clearly as to adoption. The believer now *feels* and *knows*, as in the other cases, that he is made pure. He has a consciousness of inward cleansing. The "Spirit of adoption" reveals himself as the "Spirit of holiness." These are not gratuitous statements, but the facts of experience in all Christians who have "followed on to know the Lord" until they have reached this stage of religious life. And the absence of this witness and experience is indubitable evidence that the work of interior purification has not taken place. Surely if the Spirit's office is to take of the things of Christ and show them unto us, he must witness, when the fact takes place, that "the blood of Jesus Christ, his Son, cleanseth us from all sin." This is implied in the nature of his office and work.

5. Nor are we, either according to reason or revelation, to restrict the domain of the Spirit's witnessing work to illumination, regeneration, and entire sanctification. We must extend it to every thing the Spirit does for the believer in the process of raising him to the heavenly state. Paul says, "Now we have received, not the spirit of the world, but the Spirit which is of God; that we might know

the things that are freely given to us of God." According to this teaching we are to know — not conjecture, or guess — but *know* the things, or the work God does for us. Now the Spirit does not end his work in the matter of entire purification, but leads the obedient Christian into the possession of gracious attainments that "passeth knowledge," and into realms of experiences that are described as "exceeding abundantly above all that we ask or think." To these advanced realizations the Spirit must testify as clearly as to sinfulness and purity; otherwise he does not make known "the things that are freely given to us of God." Besides, it is a fact of experience that when the soul is filled with a heavenly sweetness almost unendurable, and ready to cry out "Stay thy hand," the believer, as in the cases previously named, *feels* and *knows* that, in the scriptural sense, he is "filled with all the fullness of God."

To all this it is replied that the Scriptures do not in as many words, as in the case of adoption, declare the witness of the Spirit to all these stages of salvation, and we have no right to assume it. But they do declare all these stages in the process of salvation. They do declare the necessity of awakening, the necessity of regeneration and adoption, the necessity of entire sanctification, the necessity of "reaching forth unto those things which are before," and the necessity of being changed "from glory to glory" by a continual "following on to know the Lord." They do declare that "the things of God knoweth no man, but the Spirit of God" — that is, that these various phases and stages of the Spirit's work are not subjects of mere human cognition, but of the Spirit's revelation. They do declare that it is the Spirit's office to "guide us into all truth," to "teach us all things," and to make known to us "the things that are freely given to us of God." These all accord with experience, and teach that the Holy Spirit does witness to his own work, be that what it may.

XVIII
WALKING IN THE LIGHT

But if we walk in the light, as he is in the light, we have
fellowship one with another, and the blood of Jesus Christ
his Son cleanseth us from all sin. —I John 1. 7.

"IF WE WALK IN the light, as he is in the light" — an
antecedent condition— "we have fellowship one
with another, and the blood of Jesus Christ his
Son cleanseth us from all sin"— sequences. The
word "but" makes the text antithetical of the verse
immediately preceding, which reads, "If we say that
we have fellowship with him, and walk in darkness,
we lie, and do not the truth." This affirms that
wrong-doing is no fruitage of divine fellowship,
and cannot co-exist with it. "But," antithetically,
fellowship and cleansing are fruitage of walking
in the light; or, as the Greek present tense of the
verbs in the original will allow, a continuous
walking in the light is attended with continuous
fellowship and cleansing.

The word "walk" is here used to signify responsible
life. "Light" is used to signify holiness, as is indicated by

the phrase "as he is in the light." This discriminates it from natural, artificial, intellectual, and all other forms of light, and confines its meaning to the spiritual, or that which inheres and surrounds the Divine nature. The declaration then is that if Christians who are supposed to be in the light, or in right moral relations, are as active as they ought to be, and all their purposes and plans be projected in purity, there is intercourse between them and God, and the blood of Christ cleanses them from all sin. Now if believers, according to the best light they have and can get with due care, use their bodies and minds as they believe rational beings ought to; if they use their domestic and social relations as they judge according to the divine ordinance; if they devote their business and church life as they believe to the glory of God, and if they harbor no thoughts or imaginations that would grieve the Holy Spirit; or, in short, if by the grace of God they do the best they can at all times, in all places, and in all the various departments of life, they must walk in the light. If this be not walking in the light it cannot be done, for no one can do more than the best he knows. But it is assumed that believers can walk in the light, and it cannot, therefore, mean more than stated. God would not ask more, and could not ask less. Hence every Christian, whether learned or unlearned, rich or poor, sick or well, in all possible conditions and places, may do the best he can under his particular circumstances, and, consequently, may walk in the light.

This walking in the light is succeeded in the order of thought by fellowship with God and interior cleansing by the blood of Christ. This fellowship is a sweet and happy intercourse between the believing soul and God. This cleansing relates specifically to the removal of inherited sinward tendencies. The Greek word, *hamartia*, translated sin, is defined by Green, in his lexicon of the Greek New Testament, "cause or principle of sin, the proneness to sin, the sinful propensity." Moreover, the Greek text uses *panta harmatia*, all sin, and is, therefore, an inspired affirmation that no defilement remains concealed down deep underneath the consciousness when the blood cleanses. Hence those believers who "walk in the light, as he is in the light," ought to claim deliverance not only from all known, but from all unknown depravity; for God's "all" embraces whatever exists of evil in the heart.

Many Christians claim to walk in the light, and to enjoy this fellowship, who will not claim this cleansing because they feel the motions of sin at times. But they feel the motions of sin *because* they will not accept fully the statement of the text. The Spirit cannot witness to cleansing, nor the believer feel the cleansing, till the fact of cleansing takes place. But the fact of cleansing cannot take place without the antecedent belief. Salvation in every degree is through faith, but faith is taking God at his word, and, hence, whoever walks in the light must venture the belief authorized in the text to get clear of the motions of sin.

So after the witness of cleansing has been experienced, in all times of temptation and absence of feeling purified believers must insist, while walking in the light, that it is written, "the blood cleanseth." They must not allow their reason to enter this realm of their faith and encroach upon its prerogatives. The analysis and judgment may do their best in determining the divinity of revelation and settling the question of walking in the light; but, these questions settled, faith must not be molested in her queenly sway over the realm of revealed truths. When keen analysis enters this realm, faith recedes and sin enters, and the spiritual life suffers the "horrors of vivisection." Only keep in the light, and let faith be supreme in her own proper dominion, and no motion of sin is felt, and a sweet consciousness of purity is experienced.

It is important to note, in studying this passage, that "cleanseth" is in the present tense and conveys the idea of continual cleansing. It does not read *has* cleansed, or *will* cleanse, but *cleanseth*. It is true, if believers have been walking in the light the blood has been cleansing; and if they will continue to walk in the light the blood will continue to cleanse; but what is declared here is that the blood *now* cleanseth while they are walking in the light. It continually cleanses while they continually walk in the light; and this continual cleansing *must not involve the notion of continual uncleanness, but a continual keeping clean.* Cleanness is a quality left after impurities are removed. A dwelling is clean when all dust and uncleanness are removed, and if some agency were put in motion to prevent a return of impurity it would be kept clean. So when the Holy Spirit cleanses the heart and enters it as a purifying agency it is continually preserved in purity. Thus believers are purified, not for a year, or a month, or even an hour at a time, but moment by moment, through continuous faith in the presence and power of the indwelling Holy Spirit.

It is inattention to the fact just stated that enables Satan to ensnare many at the point where faith first apprehends an application of the cleansing blood. They are persuaded it is better not to commit themselves to the confession of purity until they test the work by various forms of prospective trial. But this is a subtle distrust of the keeping power of grace, and puts such believers in an expectancy of failure. Of course when the trials come failure takes place, for it was expected. The scriptural course is to walk in the light, claim the cleansing, and continue to claim it moment by moment while passing through the trials, and the result must be unbroken victory.

Another mistake, often proving disastrous, arises from inattention to the momentary nature of this cleansing. If purified persons should unfortunately be precipitated into sin they accept the view that they were mistaken concerning their previous state, and abandon further effort after holiness. Instead of adopting this view and course they should understand that they have lost their previous state, and that they may and ought at once to regain it by penitence and faith.

There is yet another unfortunate inference, arising from wrong views of this cleansing, which leads to the doubt whether any believer ever was or can be cleansed from all sin. When persons possessing holiness fall into wrongdoing the general verdict is that they never possessed what they claimed. The scriptural conclusion, however, is that they have ceased to walk in the light, and the blood has ceased to cleanse. It is terrible enough that a purified person should fall into sin; but that it should also produce the impression that all such claims are fanciful, and that none should aim at a complete deliverance from sin, is still more appalling.

To summarize, then: If believers will by the grace of God be honest and sincere in all their activities, thus keeping a conscience void of offense toward God and man, and continually trust Christ for all he has engaged to do for them, they shall continually have sweet fellowship with God, and the blood of his Son will continue to cleanse them from all sin. This continual trust will become such a habit of the soul that it will, like natural respiration, act without conscious volition or effort, and give believers a sense of permanent purity rather than constant cleansing. So, while they sing the familiar couplet,

"Every moment, Lord, I *need*
The merits of thy death;"

They sing also,
"Every moment, Lord, I *have*
The merits of thy death."

XIX
DELIGHT IN GOD

Delight thyself also in the Lord , and he shall give thee the desires of thine heart. —Psalm 37. 4.

THE WORD "ALSO" REFERS to a statement in the verse immediately preceding, and makes at tention to that verse necessary to a correct understanding of the passage cited. That verse reads, "Trust in the Lord, and do good; so shalt thou dwell in the land, and verily thou shalt be fed." Here is set forth a high religious state with its valuable rewards. The promise may be interpreted both temporally and spiritually. Persons trusting in the Lord and doing good are welcomed to any neighborhood, town or city; to any Church, or among any Christian people; they are good citizens and useful to any society or state; they have a sufficiency for the body, and their souls are fed by the Word, religious literature, and the means of grace. They are blessed in their relations to both worlds.

But good as is this religious state, and highly rewarded as it is, the passage selected for exposition brings forward

a more advanced state, and one rewarded in a more remarkable manner. To delight in the Lord is more than to
trust in him and to do good; and to receive the desires of
the heart is more than to dwell in the land and to be fed.
Many trust in the Lord and do good who cannot properly be said to delight in him. Many dwell in the land
and are fed, yet still have many unsatisfied desires. But
the scripture under notice affirms that whosoever delights
himself in the Lord shall have no unsatisfied craving of
the heart. Such a remarkable statement demands the closest and most prayerful study. Let us, therefore, note some
of the salient points of the passage.

1. *The desires of the heart are its longings, and are here
used by figure for the objects of these longings.* — All good
people desire correct inward states of the heart, and outward conditions favorable to these inward states. They
desire the salvation of their families, of their neighbors,
and of their fellow-citizens. They desire the sanctification
of the Church and the universal spread of the Gospel.
They desire whatever will alleviate human misery, increase
human happiness, and glorify God. Of course they are
deeply interested in the manner in which these things
are to be secured, and may find it stated in the scripture
under consideration.

2. *Delight in the Lord is here presented as the royal recipe
for all we need under the sun, and is unlike any other ever
known to man.* — All others require some expenditure of
time, or money, or unpleasant labor, or something else of
the nature of work or sacrifice; but this promise makes
sure all we desire by simply delighting ourselves — in the
Lord. It is not by endowing colleges, building churches,
feeding and clothing the poor; nor by chanting anthems
and singing psalms; nor by exercises of praise and prayer;
nor by any other conceivable form of religious work, only
so far as it may be implied in a delight in the Lord. It is a
certain state of the affections that is represented as con-

taining and exerting this strange talismanic power. It is that exquisite satisfaction and supreme delight in the Lord, which is fairly represented in New Testament teaching by the pleasure which the bride has in the bridegroom, that contains the almighty charm.

3. *It is vital to note carefully that this delight must be in the Lord himself as distinguished from his work and his people.* — Of course, whoever delights in the Lord will delight also in his worship and his worshipers; but one of the most subtle and dangerous snares of Satan is to gradually and insensibly wean the hearts of good people from the Lord and wed them idolatrously to some particular form of religious labor or some particular circle of religious laborers. Many of God's servants are nearly killed when compelled to leave their favorite work in the ranks of the effective ministry. The divinity zealously worshiped by them signally fails, and a species of weeping and wailing supervenes. Did they delight themselves as they ought in the Lord who never fails, they would remain peaceful and happy in their superannuation, and adapt themselves to some Christian work suited to their lessened strength. "Let not him that girdeth on the harness boast himself as he that putteth it off." Putting off the harness by the divine order ought to be, and, if the affections were rightly placed, would be a season of greater rejoicing than when it was girded on. Surely this is the thought of Christian progress, though it be not always the fact of experience. It is to be feared that there are many in the Church today under the fatal delusion that their attachment to some favorite form of Christian work is a delighting in the Lord; and nothing but death will break the snare and show the idolatry.

4. *It is assumed that this state of the affections is possible and volitional.* — If not possible, this scripture is mockery; if not volitional, it could not be rewardable as indicated, and is a tantalization of the believer. Hence

every Christian is responsible for his want of this supreme love to God. He is invited into such fellowship and association with the Holy Spirit as will most certainly secure this high state of grace. It might be impossible for the reader to construct a railway of even a few miles, but, invited into partnership with some railroad prince who can furnish readily all the money needed, he can build one of any length. So "we are laborers together with God." Every divine command involves a correlative promise of all necessary grace and help. In the light of this passage, then, the moral delinquency of the Church every-where apparent is truly appalling.

5. *The future tense of the promise, "He shall give," must not be referred to eternity, nor to any distant period in time to come.* — It is implied in the nature of delight in the Lord that there are no counter-currents in the soul, or that there remain no cravings of the heart which divine holiness and love dare not satisfy. Hence, the grace urged here as a present attainment must involve a present elimination of all abnormal appetites of the body and of all depraved affections of the soul, and such a tempering of all the natural appetites and desires as will not call for excess in gratification nor clamor for unlawful methods of indulgence. The interior reconstruction must be so complete that the soul will be fully harmonized with God and his government. No exception must be taken to the internal states of the heart, nor to the outward conditions of life, by those who delight themselves in the Lord; because these states and conditions, as well as every thing else affecting their interest and happiness, must be viewed as the appointments of their gracious heavenly Father. The divine dealings with them personally, with their families, with their fellow-citizens, and with the world in general, must be satisfactory to them.

In view of the actual facts of experience it might seem that this promise must have a very liberal interpretation.

For many of the most saintly persons suffer great afflictions and make the usual and proper efforts to escape from them. And the greatest desire of all purified believers is the arrest of all wickedness and the universal spread of righteousness; and this desire of the good has not been satisfied in the case of one single saint. But religious experience contains many paradoxes, of which this is one of the most interesting. The most afflicted Christian who delights in the Lord realizes an inward rest and contentment while he is making effort to escape from his sufferings. And amid the sorrow felt at the sins of the world, the purified "fret not themselves because of evil doers," and experience a sense that every craving of the heart is satisfied.

Would you, as parents, see your children convicted and converted? Delight yourself in the Lord. This will warm the atmosphere of the home circle and render attractive to the children the religion you profess. Would you lead your Sunday-school pupils to renounce sin and accept Christ? Delight yourself in the Lord. It will give such winsomeness to your spirit, talk, and movements as will draw the pupils to Jesus. Would you as pastors of churches lead the membership into deeper acquaintance with God and see sinners awakened and regenerated? Delight yourself in the Lord. This will lead you to observe with great care the apostolic counsel, "Take heed unto thyself, and unto the doctrine; continue in them: for in doing this thou shalt both save thyself, and them that hear thee."

In short, is there any point you want to reach, any object you wish to obtain, any enterprise you want to consummate; is there any unallayed craving, any unsatisfied desire, any longing not met? Adopt and use the royal recipe of the text, and thou shalt have the desires of thine heart.

Glory to the Father, glory to the Son, and glory to the Holy Ghost. Amen and Amen.

XX
CHRIST'S PUTTING OF
REGENERATION AND SANCTIFICATION

If a man love me, he will keep my words: and my Father will love him, and we will come unto him, and make our abode with him. —John 14, 23.

THIS TEXT IS TAKEN FROM what may be called the Saviour's valedictory. In this farewell address he speaks to his disciples as true Christians, and instructs them accordingly. Hence we read, "For the Father himself loveth you, because ye have loved me and have believed that I came out from God." Again, "If the world hate you, ye know that it hated me before it hated you. If ye were of the world, the world would love his own; but because ye are not of the world, but I have chosen you out of the world, therefore the world hateth you." Though the Saviour recognized the Christian character of his disciples, he affirms, at different times during his discourse, that they had not received all that the Gospel provided for them. Accordingly he says, "I will pray the Father, and he shall give you another Comforter, that he may abide with you forever;" and again, "But when the Comforter is come, whom I will send unto you from the Father, even the spirit of truth, which proceedeth from the Father, he shall testify of me." In other connections of the discourse the same statements and promises are made.

The text is a clear statement of the fact that fidelity in the first stages of religious life will be followed by more marvelous displays of saving power and interior workings of the Three in One. Let us, then, examine the Saviour's notions concerning

I. A JUSTIFIED CHRISTIAN

"If a man love me, he will keep my words," embodies the Saviour's views of a true believer; he loves God, and keeps his commandments. Whatever may be done or not done at conversion, the carnal mind, which is enmity against God and not subject to his law, is so far repressed that the happy subject of the change loves and obeys God. The Saviour's teaching, then, is,

1. *A justified Christian loves God.* — Death in trespasses and sins has been displaced by a spiritual life which shows itself in love, peace, joy, long-suffering, gentleness, goodness, etc. He delights in God, in his law, in his house, in his worship, and in his work. "His delight is in the law of the Lord; and in his law doth he meditate day and night."

It is the nature of this love for God to awaken sympathy and affection for all God's creatures, and especially for mankind. Hence a true Christian is kind to his fellows, bearing patiently, and for a long time, the injuries or wrongs which their weaknesses or sins may inflict. He does not envy any one his prosperity, usefulness or honor, but is pleased at the success of all in every legitimate enterprise. He makes all due effort, consistent with his obligations to himself and his dependents, to aid all persons, even his enemies, in their laudable undertakings. "Charity seeketh not her own." Such a person is "a new creature in Christ Jesus; old things have passed away, behold all things have become new."

It is not hinted that such a one may not, at times, feel something rising within him opposed to these graces; for this would be at variance with scripture and universal experience; but the evil within is so far subdued and kept under that the believer does not sin. Hence another item in the Saviour's teaching is,

2. *A justified Christian obeys God.*— "He will," says Jesus, "keep my words;" he studies them, keeps them in memory, and obeys them. He is a person of prayer and Christian work; he leaves nothing undone which he thinks he ought to do, and thereby keeps a conscience void of offense toward God. He walks abreast of his light, realizing that "there is no condemnation to them which are in Christ, who walk not after the flesh, but after the Spirit."

It is a fearful mistake to suppose that the initial Christian life allows any act that contracts guilt; and it is painful to think how common it is in these days to hear professors of religion confess that they do many things which they ought not to do, that they make many crooked paths, and that they feel guilt and condemnation as the result. And, with all this, they view themselves as justified believers, and ask their brethren to pray for them, that they may prove faithful and at last get to heaven! Faithfulness in such a course will certainly end in the eternal loss of the soul! The plain statement of Christ is, "If a man love me he will keep my words." Love and obedience are the inseparable marks of a justified Christian; and fidelity in this relation is succeeded, sooner or later, in every case, by deeper and sweeter intimacies with the adorable Trinity.

This brings us to notice the Saviour's ideas of,

II. AN ENTIRELY SANCTIFIED CHRISTIAN

This new experience is described by Jesus in the words, "My Father will love him, and we will come unto him, and make our abode with him." These words must mean something more, or something different, from the meaning they might have in any application that can be made of them to the initial religious life; for the Saviour is here speaking of a post-conversion experience, and an experience that succeeds to fidelity in a justified relation to God. It will not do to say that the allusion here is to the special endowments of the disciples at Pentecost, fitting them for the exigencies of their times, and the special work of organizing the Church; for the words of the text state a general proposition. "If a man love me, he will keep my words;" that is, any man, in any place, and in any period of time— "my Father will love him, and we will come unto him, and make our abode with him." The particulars of the new experience are, then,

1. *The Father's love.—* Since the Father's love for his children in every case is infinite, in the case of the entirely sanctified the Saviour must mean that faith discerns this love more clearly, and the soul enjoys it more sensibly. This interpretation is confirmed by the experience of all perfected in faith and holiness. Such Christians are as sure that God loves them as they are of their own being, or any other fact of consciousness, and enjoy it with a sweetness that no language can describe.

Since "We love him because he first loved us," our love for God will increase and intensify in the measure of our perception of the certainty and vastness of his love for us. The clear perception of his infinite love for us will be followed by the perfection of our love for him. Pure, unmixed, holy love is, therefore, one of the marks of the entirely sanctified. Another particular of the new experience as given by Jesus is,

2. *The abiding presence of the Father, Son, and Holy Spirit.*— Some eminent saints in different ages of the Church have had such intimacy in their divine communion as to discern the distinct persons of the trinity, and hold sweet intercourse with each adorable Person. But this is not general experience, nor is it necessary to the entirely sanctified state. It is enough that faith discerns clearly the indwelling of the adorable Personages in unity. This divine presence *abiding* in the soul, and uninterruptedly witnessing to believers both their pardon and purity, is graciously promised, and sensibly enjoyed in the experience of all who have become established in holiness. No matter how faintly love, at times, may be felt as an emotion, nor to what degree joy may have subsided, nor to what extent the surface of peace may be disturbed, nor what may be the character of the storm which Satan may awake around those established in this experience, the assurance of their purity remains. Their consecration to God and their present salvation, like Alpine heights, rise above all other feelings, thoughts, and facts around them. The Comforter *abides.*

This wonderful divine indwelling, when clearly discerned by their faith, brings believers consciously into the most intimate of all relations to the adorable Saviour— the relation of the bride to the bridegroom. In the consciousness of this enrapturing union, like the bride who surrenders herself and all her interests to her chosen partner and lord, believers feel that all they are, all they have, and all they can do, are handed over to Christ; and that their interests are identical— *one and inseparable* for ever and ever. No tongue can describe, no pen can picture, the blessedness of this marvelous union, under the inspiration of which Charles Wesley attempted no more than to express amazement:

"O'erwhelmed with thy stupendous grace,
   I cannot in thy presence move;
But breathe unutterable praise,
   And rapt'rous awe and silent love."

It will be seen from the Saviour's putting of this sub-ject, that the Christian life is one of love and obedi-ence; that fidelity in it is succeeded, sooner or later, by more wonderful displays of saving grace; that these displays are not indiscriminately made, but are the heritage and reward of God's faithful child; and that this sanctifying grace does no more precede nor ac-company conversion than regeneration precedes or accompanies repentance. It will be seen also from the Saviour's putting of this subject that perfected holi-ness is not distinguished from the lower religious life by the matter of obedience. The justified relation, it has been seen, requires implicit obedience; the entirely sanctified state can require no more. It is true that su-perior light and liberty enlarge the sphere and inten-sify the religious activities of the entirely sanctified, but do not distinguish it from the partially sanctified state. It is, as will appear from the Saviour's statement, more an inward experience than an outer life; and attention to these facts would stir careless professors to greater activi-ties, and would abate the severity of their criticisms upon the outward lives of the professedly holy.

Dear reader, are you of the number who know they are making crooked paths, and are not looking unto God for deliverance? If so, be alarmed and flee to Christ for refuge. Is your Christian life one of love and obedience? If so, look for the incoming of the Holy Ones to uninter-ruptedly abide with you forever. Look for this every day, every hour, every moment. Look for it now! Reckon your-self dead indeed unto sin, but alive unto God." Do this now! and as sure as God hath spoken you will sing,

"Tis done; thou dost this moment save;
  With full salvation bless;
Redemption through thy blood I have,
  And spotless love and peace."

XXI
SPIRITUAL POWER

But ye shall receive power after that the Holy Ghost is come upon you; and ye shall be witnesses unto me both in Jerusalem and in all Judea, and in Samaria, and unto the uttermost parts of the earth. —Acts 1. 8.

THIS SCRIPTURE AWAKENS in the mind three questions. First: What was the spiritual status of the apostles at the time of this address? Second: What was their spiritual want which the Pentecost was to supply? Third: For what work did the new enduement prepare them?

1. *The pre-pentecostal state of the apostles.* — First, they were truly and evangelically converted. They had left their secular business and received Christ and followed him, and, hence, had received "power to become the sons of God." They had been called together and received "power and authority over all devils, and to cure diseases," and had gone "through the towns, preaching the Gospel, and healing every-where." They surely did not do this in an unconverted state.

In his farewell address the Saviour said to them,

"If ye were of the world, the world would love his own; but because ye are not of the world, but I have chosen you out of the world, therefore the world hateth you." In his intercessory prayers the Saviour says: "I have given them Thy Word; and the world hath hated them, because they are not of the world, even as I am not of the world." All these facts can be predicated of none but converted persons.

Second, in estimating the religious character of these apostles at the time of this last address, there are other statements made concerning them that must be noticed. The Saviour frequently rebuked them for an unbelief which greatly weakened their faith. They were gross in their spiritual perceptions of the nature of Christ's kingdom, and were ambitious to occupy its chief offices. They were vindictive in their feelings, and wished to burn up a whole village and villagers.

Looking at the gracious side of these men, some have concluded that they were not only converted, but sanctified wholly. Others, viewing only their defective side, have concluded that they were not converted at all. The truth, no doubt, is, they were truly regenerated, but there remained a carnal principle antagonizing their Christian graces, and breaking out in fear, ambition, resentment, and other depraved affections.

2. *The spiritual want of the apostles in their pre-pentecostal state.*— Whatever this want was, it was to be met by the promise of the Father, or by the baptism of the Holy Ghost. From what has been said, it is clear they needed a deliverance from unbelief, from spiritual dullness, from worldly ambition, and from resentful feelings. Now, these wrong affections arose from either a depraved principle, or some weakness of their spiritual state, which could be remedied only by the Holy Spirit. Take what view we please, we cannot escape the necessity of a post-conversion work of the Spirit. But since these affections

are such as are universally found in depraved natures, they must have sprung from a depraved source in these apostles, and hence their need was the elimination of this seed of sin."

Again, they needed an enduement of power which they had not at the time. "Ye shall receive power after that the Holy Ghost is come upon you." This was not, as some teach, the power to heal diseases, cast out devils, and other miracles; for they had received this at the beginning of their ministry. It was a much greater and purer endowment; it was power to live and act upon the high moral plane of the new commandment.

Before his passion the Saviour said: "A new commandment I give unto you, that ye love one another; as I have loved you, that ye also love one another." This commandment was to take effect on and after the Pentecost, and was to embody the ethical system of the new dispensation. It was necessary, then, to obtain a purity and power to love as Jesus loved; in honor to prefer one another, to take the suffering upon themselves, and relieve others; and to lay down their lives, if called to it, for the brethren.

It was in this freedom from self-seeking, and in this strange love for others, which the apostles showed after the Pentecost, that we are to find the secret of their power over men.

Lastly, and in short, they needed the inauguration of the new dispensation in their souls. They had received the Spirit in his regenerating and adopting offices, they now needed him in his purifying and empowering offices. Hence, the Saviour said to them: "I will pray the Father, and he shall give you another Comforter, whom ye know, for he dwelleth with you, and shall be in you." The "shall be in you," called the gift of the Holy Ghost, was what they wanted.

After the resurrection, and before the ascension, the

Saviour met the eleven and breathed upon them and said, "Receive ye the Holy Ghost," and yet, with this new installment of the Spirit, they did not receive the gift of power promised. The fullness of the Holy Spirit, called the gift of the Holy Ghost, and baptism of the Holy Ghost, the thing needed, they did not receive till they "tarried," "waited," "departed not," and realized the fulfillment of "the promise of the Father."

3. *The work for which this enduement prepared them.* — "Ye shall be witnesses unto me," etc. They were not called to defend, but to declare and witness to the truth. They were to commence their testimonies in Jerusalem, their home; in their families, among their neighbors and fellow citizens. This testimony, of course, was to be rendered credible by a manifest change in life which, with the testimony, would alarm the guilty.

After witnessing at home the disciples were to extend their labors "into all Judea, Samaria, and to the uttermost part of the earth." It is a peculiarity of this wonderful grace that it gives an irrepressible desire to tell it at home and abroad. One of the obvious peculiarities of the genuine holiness meeting is the prevalence of testimony, and was a distinguishing element in the Pentecostal enduement.

In closing it will be edifying to note the form of the Spirit's visit in his empowering office. It would seem that the purging work of the Spirit, by coming into the believer and expelling impurities, is not necessarily his empowering work. Purity is power, no doubt, but not *the* power which the Christian worker must have to reach the maximum of his efficiency. Jesus was perfectly pure, and filled with the Spirit, yet, when about to enter upon his mission, he was baptized, prayed, saw heaven opened, and saw the Spirit descending and remaining upon him. Not until this did he say, "The Spirit of the Lord is upon me, because he

hath anointed me to preach the gospel to the poor,"
etc. So it seems from the text, from the Saviour's statement, and from other scripture, that the spiritual impulses which move to effective work are something
more than a sense of purity.

As our bodies may be filled with air, and at the same
time it may sweep down upon us in tornado form and
carry us away, so our souls may be filled with the Spirit,
and yet he may sweep down upon us and carry us
whithersoever he listeth. And it is this sweeping down
upon the purified believer that seems to be the Spirit's
empowering work. Here is an explanation of the weakness of many holy people. Their faith never apprehended
something like the Saviour's vision of heaven opened and
the dove descending, or the Pentecostal experience of the
rushing mighty wind and cloven tongues of fire sitting
upon them. Such should "tarry," "wait," "depart not,"
till this takes place.

XXII
THE GREAT COMMISSION

As my Father hath sent me, even so send I you. —John 20. 21.

THE PRONOUN "MY," which the reader will notice is in *Roman*, indicating that it was inserted by the translators, may be omitted without "taking away from the words of the prophecy of this book." Its insertion in the text widens the circle of the Saviour and his apostles, and seems to indicate that they belonged to different families and had different paternities. But dropping it the circle is contracted, and they are brought into the most intimate domestic relations with a common Fatherhood. And the omission of this pronoun in the original text clearly indicates the Saviour's purpose and meaning at the time. "As the Father hath sent me, even so send I you." Thus he would have them feel that they were all of one family, with a common Father and a common interest, and he would have all Christian workers of to-day feel the same intimate relationship and move under the same sweet inspiration.

A more important matter is discovered in the tenses of the verbs used by our Lord. "As the Father hath sent me " is in a past tense, and indicates a finished fact; but, "so send I you" is in the Greek present tense, and indicates a continuous act. The Lord would have the disciples understand that their call and commission were as much by the moment, and as constantly dependent upon their loyalty, as their spiritual life itself. This life in the soul begins with a self-surrendering faith in God and an acceptance of Christ as a personal Saviour, and continues while this faith and submission last. So the call and commission to preach and prophesy continues, or is continually renewed, while the moral relations with God are correct and preserved intact. But should self-seeking, or any ambitious scheme, or any other perverse measure, disturb these relations, the Saviour cannot continue to say, "so send I you." Hence all Christian laborers should carefully guard their inward spiritual states, that they might always hear, and might always feel, the enthusiasm of the utterance, "As the Father hath sent me, even so send I you." This passage is applied in this article indiscriminately to ministerial and lay workers, because the New Testament idea of a Christian Church is that all the members— from the pastor, who is the official head, down to the humblest member— are prophets, and may, in their appropriate spheres, "speak unto men to edification, exhortation, and comfort," and consequently need the same divine enduement.

Many are working with all their might in the pulpits and pews, and wondering why they have no success, while others, with much less talent and effort, are gathering large harvests into the churches. The secret is, their commission was long ago forfeited through unfaithfulness in some form, and has not been renewed, and cannot be till they change their attitude by a new consecra-

XXII: THE GREAT COMMISSION **141**

tion of themselves to God. The commission of some years ago will no more serve for the present than the blessing of some years ago will serve the soul's present wants. As the soul must have a present blessing to meet its present needs, so the religious worker, whether minister or layman, must have a present whisper of the words, "As the Father hath sent me, even so send I you," or failure is inevitable. Whoever, therefore, would be a successful worker in the vineyard of the Lord must keep his moral relations with God and man properly adjusted, and feel assured that his call and commission are in process of continued renewal.

Another point of paramount importance, and demanding a more extensive notice, is the Saviour's transfer of his own personal endowments to his chosen workers, thereby making their mission a duplicate and extension of his own. "As the Father hath sent me, even so send I you," with the same protection against failure, with the same promises of success, and the same divine qualifications for constant and final victory. Before the Father ordered the Son upon his mission he sent him to John at the Jordan to receive baptism by water, and in this he received the Holy Ghost in his empowering offices. Jesus was always pure, and was filled with the Spirit from his birth; but he did not enter upon his divine work till he received the Holy Spirit in his anointing or working power. It was this which gave to our Lord the adorable title of CHRIST, an untranslated Greek word, meaning "The Anointed One," and authorized him to declare in the synagogue of Nazareth, "The Spirit of the Lord is upon me, because he hath anointed me to preach the Gospel to the poor; he hath sent me to heal the broken-hearted," and so on.

In accordance with these facts, and his promise in the text, the Saviour commanded his disciples, both apostles and laymen, male and female, "that they should not depart from Jerusalem, but wait for the promise of the Father." He had previously ordered the apostles to go into all the world and preach the Gospel to every creature, and now he gives a complementary order to tarry until they were endued with power from on high. A failure, therefore, to tarry for the enduement would have been as sad and fatal as the failure to go. Both were equally binding, and made a complete whole. The command to tarry was obeyed by all the disciples, and they issued from the upper chamber purified and empowered — the apostles to execute their great commission, the others to perform the subordinate work; and their first effort was crowned with three thousand additions to the Spirit-baptized company. From this time onward they indulged no more self-seeking, no more disputing who should be the greatest, no more resentment when slighted or abused, no more depraved affections of any kind; but, on the contrary, they knew nothing but Christ and him crucified," and laid down at his feet all personal ease, all their powers, all their dearest rights, and even life itself, for the advancement of his cause and the spread of his glory.

These facts were to shadow forth the divine policy and the character and qualifications of evangelical laborers through all the future ages. And now, when the Saviour calls workers to the fields of Gospel toil, he orders them to tarry until they become Christians in the full New Testament sense, or in such union with himself that they receive, like the branch from the vine, his light, his life, his unction, his power, and every other Christly quality. This happens when the believer, under the illuminations of regenerating grace and the adopting Spirit, puts away every thing which he believes offensive to God, and accepts all the divine will, and receives Christ for all he has engaged to do for the Christian, and experiences what is called the baptism of the Holy Ghost. Without this no one can be an efficient worker in any department of religious toil. The highest forms of morality, the best common phases of Christianity, the noblest gifts of the colleges, and the profoundest instruction of the theological schools, however important as helps, cannot make effective laborers in the vineyard of the Lord. Nothing short of the unction of the Holy One will answer. Paul said, in speaking to this point, "Our sufficiency is of God, who also hath made us able ministers of the new testament; not of the letter, but of the Spirit; for the letter killeth, but the Spirit giveth life."

The inference, therefore, is inevitable, that any gracious state short of the fullness of the Spirit is ineligibility to the ministries of the Church, and that the Saviour appoints none to them, according to our text, unless their moral character is such that he can transfer to them the anointing which he received of the Father. "As the Father hath sent me, even so send I you." It is sheer mockery of the poor, and a re-opening of the wounds of the brokenhearted, to go to them with the mere letter of the Gospel without the Spirit; but when the messenger can say, as he may and ought, "The Spirit of the Lord is upon me, because he hath anointed me to preach the Gospel to the poor," and so on, the heart is reached, the message is received, the solace is administered, the captive is delivered, the bruised are freed, and the acceptable year of the Lord is ushered in. With such a call and commission as are here promised a failure is as impossible as that Christ himself should fail. He becomes the continued complement of his servant, and what the servant has not in himself he has in his Lord; and as He said, "The living Father hath sent me, and I live by the Father," so the servant can say, "The living Christ hath sent me, and I live, and labor, and triumph through him."

The inferences are easily drawn and full of inspiration and cheer. First, we should feel ourselves drawn into the most intimate relations with Jesus and each other in Christian work.

Second, we should carefully keep our moral relations correct, and expect the constant whisper, "As the Father hath sent me, so send I you."

Third, we should proceed to our work during our loyalty with the assumption that our Lord's anointing rests upon us, and our success an absolute certainty.

XXIII
THE MINISTERIAL GIFT

Neglect not the gift that is in thee, which was given thee by prophecy, with the laying on of the hands of the presbytery. —I Tim. 4. 14.

THE GIFT REFERRED TO may be defined, in few words, to be ministerial power. It is a divine qualification, as we learn from the preceding context, to read with proper emphasis and exposition the sacred Scriptures, to exhort and move the people to obedience, and to teach the way of duty in matters concerning which there is no specific revelation. This qualification consists of a supernatural light, which reveals the spiritual significance of the word, a divine readiness and liberty in communicating this meaning to others, and a divine breath which carries the utterances to the hearts of hearers and makes them feel that the messages are from God. It is not bestowed by the colleges of science, nor the seminaries of theology, but it is a holy consecration of all natural and acquired abilities to the work of God, and exercised by the supernaturally vitalized mental and moral forces of the workers.

1. *The gift in question is said to be conferred "by prophecy, with the laying on of the hands of the presbytery"* — There had been some prophecies uttered, perhaps before the birth of Timothy, pointing to him and his evangelistic mission; and some commentators think that the reference of the text is to those prophecies. But in the opening of the epistle (chap. 1. 18), where the apostle evidently alludes to Timothy's commission as a fulfillment of some former prophecies, he uses *kata* with the accusative and the plural form of the noun, properly translated "according to the prophecies." In the text he uses *dia* with the genitive and the singular form of the noun, indicating medium or instrumentality. Hence the apostle intends to say that through the medium of a prophecy, uttered in connection with the ceremony of laying on of hands, Timothy received the gift of ministerial power.

The author of this epistle in his first letter to the Corinthians (chap. 14. 3) defines prophesying to mean, "speaking unto men to edification, exhortation, and comfort." It would, therefore, seem that at the installation of Timothy into the office of an evangelist an address had been made to him corresponding to what is known in Methodist circles as the Bishop's address to the candidates for deacons' or elders' orders. This address and imposition of hands, in the case of Timothy, was more than an official recognition of his induction into the ministerial office. It was also a divinely appointed channel for the communication of the heavenly unction which that office needed. So the Bishop's address of to-day and the laying on of the hands of the elders ought to be viewed, both by those who administer and those who receive the rite, as more than mere official recognition. They should expect large communications of the Holy Ghost through this heaven-ordained medium.

2. *This gift may be neglected; and hence Timothy was most solemnly guarded against such a fatal mistake.* — The most common way of neglecting any gift is by disuse; but no preacher in the regular work can neglect the ministerial gift in this way while he is exercising it weekly, and often daily. In the succeeding context Paul indicates the manner in which this neglect might be practiced; namely, by failing to think closely upon ministerial work, and not giving one's self wholly to it. The order to Timothy, according to the Greek text, is, to exist, or to live, within the circle of ministerial duties; to let no part of himself get without this circle; to connect no other enterprise or business with it; but to get all his inspiration, his happiness and support through undivided attention to his evangelistic work.

Whoever will fully consecrate himself to God, and shall be called to this work and give himself wholly to it, will find no necessity in calling to his aid any secular business for his support. Paul gave the churches of his day to understand that tent-making was not a necessity with him but a choice, at the time and under the circumstances, lest the Gospel might be blamed. Had it been best for all concerned, and most for the glory of God, that Paul should have spent all his time in the direct work of soul-saving, God would have moved the people to his support. But in view of all the interests to be served, and the bearing of his course upon the future Church, it was best to adopt at the time the self-supporting policy. Hence, tent-making with Paul was as much a work of soul-saving as going with tears from house to house with the messages of life, and, so far from being a neglect of his gift, was proper attention to it. So it is with the truly consecrated lay or local preacher of the Churches in all times. But no such principles apply to what is technically called the effective ministry, nor can any such apology be made for any step that would secularize the pulpit.

3. *Another fact inferable from the text, and clearly stated in another place, is that this heavenly gift may be lost.*— In closing this epistle Paul most touchingly writes, "O, Timothy, keep that which is committed to thy trust, avoiding profane and vain babblings, and oppositions of science falsely so-called; which some professing have erred concerning the faith." In this tender caution the apostle indicates the most common and dangerous ways of losing ministerial power. They are: secular talk, vain conversation, questionable witticisms and repartee, jesting that is not convenient, telling anecdotes which do not tend to godliness, reading trashy literature, and whatever else may be comprehended in "vain babblings." Another way is by the use of what he terms "oppositions of science falsely so-called"— the antithesis of gnosis.

The *gnosis* seems to have been the dogmas, theories, and philosophic systems, whose supporters claimed for them the embodiment of true knowledge, while they were, at best, admixtures of truth and error. The *antitheses* were the logical statements which disproved the claims of the theories and systems, and were meritorious and proper in their place, but dangerous weapons in the hands of those whose whole business was to know nothing but Christ and him crucified. Hence the preachers of that day who studied these philosophic systems and professed an acquaintance with the *antitheses*, or methods of disproval, erred concerning the faith.

This history has repeated itself in every age of the Christian Church. As a matter of fact the preachers of this day who yield to the witchery of such study, and drag it into their pulpits, not only scatter a poisonous skepticism among the people, but dissipate all their own spirituality and become as dry and lifeless as mummies. Besides, it is not long after this course is adopted till such preachers discover that some parts of the Old Scriptures are not canonical, that some parts of the New are uninspired, and thus start on a down grade to utter apostacy. Professing acquaintance with the different phases of materialistic philosophy, and professing ability to answer them like their prototypes of apostolic times, they err concerning the faith.

It is not doubted that God calls men now and then, as Fletcher, in Wesley's day, and Joseph Cook, of our own day, to demolish by scientific methods the different phases of philosophic and theological error, but nine hundred and ninety-nine out of every thousand are called to declare and witness to the truth and let its logical defense alone. The best possible defense of the truth of God which ministers can make, even the Fletchers and Cooks of the Church, is witnessing, by the conscious inworking of the Holy Spirit, to the truths they declare. Nothing so thoroughly closes the mouths of skeptics and silences the batteries of infidelity.

4. *Another fact inferable from the text and clearly stated in the second epistle is that this gift, tender and delicate as it is, may be retained.* — In the second letter to Timothy (chap. 1. 14) we read: "That good thing which was committed to thee keep by the Holy Ghost which dwelleth in us." Here it is seen that this divine gift can be retained only while the Holy Spirit dwells in its possessor. This is because the gift is nothing more or less than the Holy Spirit himself working on the line of saving souls through the natural and acquired abilities of the minister. Hence, to keep the gift, the minister must so guard his physical, intellectual, domestic, social, and private life as not to grieve the Holy Spirit. He must preach the highest standard of purity known to him; his private, public, and professional life must be fully up to that standard; he must daily seek to know more of God and his word, and must constantly walk fully abreast of his ever-increasing light. Any thing short of this will grieve the Spirit and weaken ministerial power. Hence the solemn caution

which stands closely connected with the text: "Take heed to thyself, and the doctrine, continue in them, for in doing this thou shalt save both thyself and them that hear thee." This is a charge to guard the appetites and instincts, lest they lead to excess and impurity; to guard the thoughts, lest ambitious aims and self-seeking find a place in the heart; to guard the preaching, lest politics, history, philosophy, or something else foreign to direct soul- saving creep into the pulpit; to see that the order, "Preach the word," be executed; and to observe every thing else necessary to personal holiness and ministerial efficiency.

Two results are positively promised upon the conditions named in this charge; first, the minister will keep constantly saved himself; and, second, he will save them that hear him. Now, if the preacher do not save them that hear him, the fearful presumption is that he does not take heed to himself and the teaching, and therefore does not save himself. Hence a failure to save others ought to alarm every minister of the Gospel.

5. *Finally, this gift may be increased in power and efficiency.* — Closely connected with the text is the order, "Meditate upon these things, give thyself wholly to them, that thy profiting may appear to all" — that is, that thy progress in personal holiness and ministerial efficiency may be clearly seen by all observers. Many preachers have their sunniest days in their early ministry, but this ought not so to be. Personal experience in divine things and success in labor ought to become more and more marked and satisfactory as the years pass, until the physical and mental powers give way under disease or age.

In the second letter (chap. 1. 6) Paul writes: "Wherefore, I put thee in remembrance that thou stir up the gift of God which is in thee." The word rendered "stir up" is one of overflowing significance, being composed of three other words meaning, respectively, intense, living, and fire. Thus the apostle assumes that the gift in question may be stirred to an intense, living flame of life, love and power. In connection with this remembrancer the method is given: "Be not thou, therefore, ashamed of the testimony of our Lord, nor of me his prisoner; but be thou partaker of the afflictions of the gospel according to the power of God." The preacher must, therefore, take heed to himself and preserve a clear, deep, sweet experience, and not be ashamed to confess it upon any proper occasion, and especially in connection with the preaching of the word. There must be no ambiguity, or rounding of the corners, to escape criticism or persecution. Nor must there be any hesitancy to stand at the side, and become identified with, Christ's little ones who may be suffering persecution for righteousness' sake. It is necessary to suffer the afflictions of the gospel, or whatever loyalty to the truth may incur, and that to such a degree, if occasion require, as shall be according to the power of God.

It will be seen from the Scriptures quoted that true ministerial power is a divine gift; that such is its purity it cannot co-exist with a careless and divided life; that personal purity is necessary to its preservation; and that to intensify its power there must be rigid loyalty to Christ in all things, at all times, and in all circumstances, under constantly increasing light. Well did the apostle cry: "Who is sufficient for these things?"

XXIV
COMMENCING WORK PREMATURELY

And he looked this way and that way, and when he saw
that there was no man, he slew the Egyptian, and hid
him in the sand. —Ex. 2. 12.

IT IS NO UNCOMMON THING for those whom God calls
to the ministry to have a divine impression in
early years that this is to be their life-work. So
it seems to have been with Moses. Hence, in his defense before the council at Jerusalem, Stephen said:
"When he was full forty years old, it came into his
heart to visit his brethren the children of Israel. And
seeing one suffer wrong, he defended him, and
smote the Egyptian: for he supposed his brethren
would have understood how that God by his hand
would deliver them; but they understood not." He
was satisfied that he was called to this work, that
he was now ready for its execution, and that his
brethren were ready to recognize him and co-oper-
ate in their deliverance, and proceeded to strike the
first blow.

This move of Moses was premature; yet it was

prompted by many considerations of great weight in the view of human reason. He "was grown," "was full forty years old," "was learned in all the wisdom of the Egyptians," "was mighty in words and deeds," "supposed his brethren understood," and knew that this work was committed to him. But he needed one of the most important and necessary qualifications; one without which all others, however numerous and great, must utterly fail. He needed a vision of God, and the inward divine voice, "My presence shall go with you;" he needed the assurance that he was now ready, and that now was the time for God to judge Egypt and deliver Israel. Without this vision and knowledge he was cowardly, and disqualified for his high mission. Hence, before he slew the Egyptian, "he looked this way and that way," fearing he might lose the favor or incur the displeasure of some persons. And when he learned, the next day, that his exploit was known he "feared," saying, "Surely this thing is known," and fled from the country and dwelt in the land of Midian.

Many who are impressed that their mission is to call sinners to repentance enter college, master the curriculum, go to the theological seminary, and issue laden with the honors of the schools, and, as with Moses, "it comes into their hearts" to enter upon their work before they have "tarried until endued with power from on high." They are "grown," they are "learned in all the wisdom" of the schools, they are "mighty in words" if not in deeds, they suppose "the brethren" understand that they are to be leaders, and they are sure the voice, "Go ye into all the world," has reached them. Besides, a perishing world is loudly calling for help, thousands are perishing daily, the mass of church members are spiritual invalids and unable to labor, "the harvest truly is great, but the laborers are few," and the call for laborers waxes louder and louder; surely they should hasten to work. But no sooner do they commence than they feel the inward impulse to "look this way and that way," lest they lose a smile or incur a frown, and when they hear of any unfavorable criticism they fear, and, instead of going to some place alone with God, they flee from duty and compromise with the formalism of the times and continue the fruitless toil. They need such an inward assurance of their divine commission and God's presence with them as will stoutly resist the temptation to self-seeking, to all ambitious schemes for place and position, to all efforts after human applause or to avoid human censure, and will set the face like a flint against all worldliness and sin.

Though Moses "was full forty years old," was "learned," was "mighty," and though the chosen people were suffering the lash of Pharaoh's task-masters among the brick-kilns of Egypt, yet God could wait forty years more, until his servant could be disciplined at the "back-side of the desert," and get a lesson without which all others were useless. This lesson consisted of various branches which all God's ministers ought to prayerfully study and apply, and which will now be briefly noted.

First, there was, no doubt, a deep and painful mortification of the self-life. Instead of an honorable court-life made up of "mighty words and deeds," instead of receiving the homage of courtiers at home and from abroad, and enjoying the brilliant society of royalty, he was a lone wanderer in a strange land, and at last became an inmate of Jethro's household and the shepherd of his flock. This employment, in the estimation of his Egyptian training, must have been the most humiliating of all work; "for every shepherd is an abomination to the Egyptians."

Next, here in the solitude of the desert, far away from the glitter and excitement of princely surroundings, with self laid in the dust, he learned in the burning and unconsumed bush what Egypt's most gifted masters could not teach him. As he "turned aside to see the great sight " he got the lesson that "our God is a consuming fire," dwelling among his people, purging them and yet not consuming them; that all who tread His courts must do it with "unshod feet" and "covered face;" and that spotless purity is a necessity to all who would lead God's people.

Another important part of the lesson at Horeb was his own utter helplessness. When he received with clear voice the order, "Come now, therefore, and I will send thee unto Pharaoh," he replied, "Who am I, that I should go unto Pharaoh, and that I should bring forth the children of Israel out of Egypt?" "But behold they will not believe me, nor hearken unto my voice." How different from the Moses of forty years before, who "supposed that his brethren would have understood" that he was their divinely-appointed deliverer! And when God encouraged him by the promise, "Certainly I will be with thee;" and by declaring his most gracious title, one comprehending all the others, and the equivalent of a blank check to be filled out at pleasure and to any amount, I AM; when he changed a rod into a serpent, and back again into a rod; when he made his hand as "leprous as snow," and changed it back again as "his other flesh;" and when he promised other miraculous endowments, if needed, Moses still pleads, "O my Lord, I am not eloquent, neither heretofore, nor since thou hast spoken to thy servant." What a difference in the man, to get away from the pride and self-conceit of the schools, from the pomp and show of court-life, and dwell in the flesh-subduing presence of God at Horeb!

There was another exercise which Moses had to pass through to complete the crucifixion of self and fully equip him for his mission. This took place on the way to his work. "And it came to pass by the way in the inn, that the Lord met him, and sought to kill him. Then Zipporah took a sharp stone, and cut off the foreskin of her son, and cast it at his feet, and said. Surely a bloody husband art thou to me. So he let him go; then she said, A bloody husband thou art, because of the circumcision." It seems that Moses had spared the feelings of his Ethiopian wife and neglected the circumcision of his son; but now, since he enters upon a great work of God, every thing must be right in his own family, and the wife must submit to the bloody ordeal. This was such a shock to Zipporah that she seems to have returned to her father's house, and saw her husband no more until he entered the wilderness of Sinai as the honored leader of the hosts of Israel. With this last experience, which was the final death-pang of the self-life, Moses was prepared to execute the divine orders how much soever it might pain himself and others dearly beloved by him.

What the Christian ministry of to-day needs is a training at the "backside of the wilderness." Horeb is the starting-point for all laborers in general evangelization, or any of the offices of the Church. The schools of science and seminaries of theology are important, but they are not adequate to the task of preparing for the ministries of the Church. They cannot teach their pupils how to tread "holy ground" with "unshod feet" and "covered face;" they cannot impart proper views of human worthlessness and the absolute necessity of divine aid in all Christian work; they cannot give forth the voice, "I am come down to deliver," "Certainly I will be with thee," "I will be thy mouth;" they cannot give the boldness to insist upon the circumcision of all her children, however much it may wound the feelings of the professing Church; and, in short, they have no vision of the burning bush and of God. For these things we must all go to the backside of the desert, and come to the mountain of God, even to Horeb." O for the humbled hearts, the disciplined affections, the chastened spirits, the softened voices, the subdued wills, the enlightened understandings, and empowered faculties, gained in loneliness with God at the "backside of the desert."

XXV
THE HOLY ANOINTING OIL

Upon man's flesh shall it not be poured; neither shall ye make any other like it, after the composition of it: it is holy, and it shall be holy unto you. Whosoever compoundeth any like it, or whosoever putteth any of it upon a stranger, shall even be cut off from his people.
—Ex. 30. 32, 33.

THE NEUTER PRONOUN "it," so frequently used in this passage, stands for the holy anointing oil. This holy oil was compounded according to a divine formula given by God to Moses. The ingredients were carefully named, the proportions were specifically stated, and the mixture was made with great exactness— "after the art of the apothecary." One of the uses of this holy compound was, by sprinkling it upon them, to sanctify the tabernacle and its sacred furniture, so that whatever touched them was made holy. But its chief use was, by pouring it upon them, to anoint priests and kings at their induction into office, and was the outward and visible sign of the impartation of such divine light, wisdom, and other qualifications as were needed for priestly intercession and the exercise of royal prerogatives.

There were certain very rigid laws regulating the use of this holy unction, and they are stated in our text. It was not to be poured upon man's flesh; it was not to be used in any secular way, nor for any secular purpose; it was not to be counterfeited or imitated in any manner, and it was not to be put upon a stranger. The last-named two offenses were particularly odious, and punishable by excision from the people of God. Now this holy oil, and the laws governing its use, have their antitypes in actual Christian life under the New Testament dispensation.

The holy oil was a type of the Holy Spirit; and its sprinkling upon the tabernacle and its vessels, so sanctifying them that whatever touched them was made holy, prefigured the saving presence of the Holy Spirit in the New Testament Church, the sacred character of all her ordinances and means of grace, and the purity of all who would dare touch them. As the tabernacle and its furniture were used for nothing but holy purposes, so church edifices, with their appendages of pulpits and pews, should be used solely for the worship of the Triune God. These buildings are dedicated to this purpose and become the dwelling-places of the Shekinah; and to use them in any secular way is to grieve the Spirit, dissipate veneration for the ordinances of religion, and gradually open the house of God for every thing unbecoming such a place. Scientific discourses from the pulpit are easy introductions of humorous lectures and burlesques to the same place. These in turn may be followed by theatricals of various kinds, and these by fairs, festivals, lotteries, and almost every other abomination. The facts of our day are the melancholy and incontrovertible proofs of the correctness of these statements. "It is holy, and it shall be holy unto you."

This unction, with its sweet spices of myrrh and cassia and sweet calamus and sweet cinnamon, beautifully symbolized the Holy Spirit's freedom from acerbity and bitterness, and his redolence with love, peace, joy, long-suffering, gentleness, goodness and every other sweet grace. No censoriousness, murmuring, fault-finding, complaining, or any other affection or practice containing the elements of sourness, can spring from the inworkings of the Holy Spirit. They are miserably out of the way whose rebukes are insults, whose fidelity takes the form of ferocity, and whose carefulness to be true has become coarseness.

As God intends all his children to be kings and priests even in this present life, the application of the holy anointing oil to these characters indicated the duty and privilege of all believers, under the new dispensation, to receive and exercise the gift of the Holy Ghost.

No Christian can govern his family with that sweetness and power, nor instruct his children with that correctness and grace, nor intercede for them with that high priestly energy which the head of every Christian family ought to exercise, until anointed of the Spirit. No preacher of the Gospel can evangelically edify and instruct, nor can he discipline and govern, nor effectually intercede for the Church of God, until he is baptized by the Holy Ghost. The same must be substantially said of Sunday-school teachers, temperance workers, missionary laborers, and all others who in any manner toil in the vineyard of the Lord. The anointing of the Spirit is a supreme necessity.

For the distribution of her charities among the beneficiary widows the Pentecostal Church demanded "men of honest report, full of the Holy Ghost and wisdom." And for the more spiritual work and exercises, of course, no less qualifications could be allowed. The Apostolic Church was no less particular. This appears in the fact that she hurried all her converts into the Pentecostal grace, and in the fact that her apostles, prophets, evangelists, pastors and teachers were given "for the perfecting of the saints," and, of course, had the qualification for this work. That the post-Apostolic Church, therefore, should have ever reached a condition admitting to her pulpits, and other official posts, persons of less qualifications than the "fullness of the Holy Ghost and wisdom" is to be greatly deplored. Indeed, the terrible failure in saving the race and populating heaven, and the wide-spread disasters which are to be felt through time and eternity, caused by this blunder, entitle it to be called *the great mistake of all the ages*.

This holy oil was not to be poured upon man's flesh. Hence kings were crowned and robed, and priests put on their miters and sacred garments, before the anointing oil was applied. Moreover, it was not applied to these officials by sprinkling, as it was to the tabernacle and its appendages, lest it might fall upon the flesh, but was poured upon their heads and ran down upon the long-flowing beard and garments, as in the case of Aaron. Now man's flesh is the divinely chosen symbol of the carnal principle; and the prohibition to touch it with the holy oil teaches that the anointing of the Spirit cannot precede the crucifixion of the self-life. This is a great practical truth too generally overlooked by believers seeking the gift of the Holy Ghost. Many cry unto the Lord for this anointing, and protract it for months, without success, and wonder at their failure. The secret is, they continue to indulge selfish plans, ambitious schemes, or something which feeds the self-life and preserves the carnal principle. While this is the case the unction cannot be applied. "Upon man's flesh shall it not be poured."

It is preposterous to seek the gracious state set forth by this holy anointing for selfish ends, as for the sole purpose of personal happiness, or mere personal success in any Christian work. The divine command is, "Be ye holy," not because it comports with religious profession, not because it inspires with happiness, not because it will make a successful minister of the Gospel or an efficient Christian laborer in some other department of religious work, but "Be ye holy; FOR I AM HOLY." Hence all secular plans, purposes and arrangements must be excluded from the exercise of seeking the incoming of the Comforter. "It is holy, and it shall be holy unto you."

Another law governing the use of the holy anointing oil prohibited any imitation of it, upon pain of excision from the people of God. The truth thus shadowed forth is terrible in its application, and especially in this day of learning, when the discipline of the schools can so nearly imitate the earnestness which the Holy Spirit awakens in the soul; for mere oratory and a zeal for some religious sect may stir up an enthusiasm indistinguishable by the masses from the operations of the Spirit upon a speaker. So, also, culture and self-control may exhibit such suavity of manners and urbanity in deportment as may be readily taken for the gentleness and long-suffering which are engendered by the Holy Spirit.

It is to be feared that there are to-day many in Christian pulpits, and other offices of the Church, whose private life and character are wrong, and who know themselves destitute of a divine unction, but substitute for it the products of culture and fruits of oratory. This is a high offense against God, as it is high-handed hypocrisy and a flagrant misrepresentation of the graces of the Spirit. It is a crime against society, as it spreads a spurious religion and misleads and ruins the unwary. O ye that substitute these products of culture and elocution for the graces of the Spirit and the gift of the Holy Ghost, stop and think before ye go further! "Whosoever compoundeth any like it shall even be cut off from his people."

This holy oil was not to be put upon a stranger. In the Mosaic vocabulary a stranger was a person not belonging to the Abrahamic family, and, therefore, ineligible to the sacred offices of priest and king. This types the idea that adoption into the household of faith must precede the gift of the Holy Ghost, that justification and regeneration must precede entire sanctification, that a deliverance from Egypt must precede an entrance into Canaan, and that a birth into the divine family must precede the anointing to kingship in that family. But it types another idea of fearful import in its practical application. As it was treason to anoint an alien, so it is excision from the spiritual Israel to place, by vote or otherwise, in the sacred offices and ministries of the Church, persons destitute of the Spirit of God and under the control of the carnal man, however fine their culture and high their moral excellences. This places a mighty emphasis upon the holy care with which the functionaries of the Church should choose their successors. O that these laws regulating the use of the holy anointing oil were conspicuously posted before every Quarterly and Annual Conference of Methodism, and before every Presbytery and Synod of the other evangelical churches!

XXVI
PROPHESYING

Despise not prophesyings. —I Thess. 5. 20.

THE WORD PROPHESY in some of its modifications is found in a great many passages both of the Old and New Scriptures. This prominence of the word indicates that the idea which it represents is important in the system of revealed truth, and ought, therefore, to be carefully studied. Most Bible readers, however, assuming that the word always means foretelling future events, pass over it too hastily for the thought its importance demands. The object of this sketch is to present the vital relation of this subject to personal holiness, and to the efficiency and aggressive work of the Church. Notice,

THE NATURE OF PROPHESYING.

The Hebrew word for prophesy in the Old Scriptures signifies "to bubble forth like a fountain," and fitly represents the act of uttering or pouring forth sacred and holy truth. The corresponding word of the

New Testament is of Greek origin, and signifies "speaking for another, or interpreting the sayings of another," and hence fitly represents the act of making known the divine mind. Note then,

1. *It means teaching.* — Teaching important truths under the illumination and guidance of the Holy Spirit. With this signification it is used in the first inspired account we have of its exercise. In the book of Numbers, 11. 24-29, there is a very interesting narrative of the early exercise of this gift, in which it is seen that it took place under special effusions of the Spirit; that it led to what the uninstructed regarded as an alarming irregularity which they asked to have suppressed; that Moses, who understood the matter, so far from discouraging it expressed a wish "that all the Lord's people were prophets;" and that prophesying here meant perceiving and teaching, by an unction from the Holy One, such truths as involved the social, civil, and religious interests of the people.

The New Scriptures seem to contract the meaning somewhat, and apply it to the impartation of religious truths alone. Hence the apostle says, I Cor. 14. 3, "But he that prophesieth speaketh unto men to edification, exhortation and comfort." This is doubtless the sense in which the apostle uses the word in the text, and means such *teachings, exhortations,* and *words of comfort* as one may utter under the anointing of the Holy Spirit. Observe,

2. *It is a gift distinct from the grace of charity.* — A person may love God and man and, therefore, enjoy true religion, and yet not be in possession of the gift of prophecy. Hence the apostle exhorts the brethren at Corinth, I Cor. 14. 1, to "Follow after charity, and desire spiritual gifts, but rather that ye may prophesy." He urges their first attention to charity, because it is of paramount importance, but he would have them add to it the gift of prophecy. So in verse 39 of the same chapter he utters the positive command, "covet to prophesy." Thus it is repre-

sented as a gift to be coveted and sought after by those who already enjoy the love of God, and, therefore, has a distinctive character.

So distinct is this gift from the grace of charity that revelation furnishes instances of persons who have in some mysterious way retained the gift and exercised it, at least on some occasions, after they had disjointed right relations with God and lost their piety. King Saul and Balaam may be referred to as instances. And there is ground for the dreadful apprehension that there are thousands to-day who once were created anew in Christ Jesus, and received a divine commission to call men to repentance, and who through ambition and worldliness have lost their piety, but, like Balaam, have retained something of the prophetic gift which they now mistake for evidence of their acceptance with God. Of these the terrible prediction is written, "Many will say unto me in that day, Lord, Lord, have we not prophesied in thy name? and in thy name have cast out devils? and in thy name done many wonderful works?" and hear in reply, "Depart from me, ye that work iniquity."

Though this Scripture and others teach the distinctive character of the gift in question, yet in many cases it is evidently conferred synchronically with converting and sanctifying grace. For often, as a matter of fact, young converts and newly sanctified Christians have special light, freedom and power in leading others to the cross. But it is also a matter of undoubted experience that this special illumination and aptness in teaching others is not always imparted at conversion or entire sanctification. Moreover, it seems that this gift is often lost by Christians while their relation to God remains undisturbed; and the consequent and unusual quietness upon subjects of religion awakens the suspicion among their brethren that they have backslidden, while the losers themselves are often unable to explain the strange experience. But whether the gift has been lost, or never been communicated, its absence lays every Christian under obligation to seek it. "Covet to prophesy."

3. *This gift may be possessed and exercised by all Christians.* — Many labor under the error that those alone, who have received special training for the business, may "speak unto men to edification, exhortation, and comfort." But it is the divine arrangement under the gospel economy that Joel's prophecy may have a literal and practical fulfillment. "I will pour my spirit upon all flesh; and your sons and your daughters shall prophesy, your old men shall dream dreams, your young men shall see visions; and also upon the servants and upon the handmaids in those days will I pour out my Spirit," Joel 2. 28-29; and Peter adds, Acts 2. 18, "and they shall prophesy." This embraces all of every age, sex, and condition in life. "Your sons shall prophesy" — not only the son educated and otherwise qualified for the pulpit, but the son in the office, the son on the farm, and the son in the work-shop — all shall prophesy. "Your daughters shall prophesy" — not only the daughter skilled in music, painting, and other fine arts shall prophesy, but all the other daughters less favored shall be endowed with the same mysterious power. Young men incompetent to search the word shall learn the mind of God in visions; and old men, disqualified by the loss of sight to consult the written oracles, shall receive divine communications in dreams, and both shall prophesy. Even the menservants who groom the horses and spade the gardens, the servant girls who cook the meals and wash the dishes, shall be filled with the Spirit, and "they shall prophesy." While, therefore, the more educated and refined should exercise this gift in their higher circles of usefulness, the lowly and uncultured should use the same wonderful endowment in their humbler spheres.

In this remarkable prophecy of Joel there is found the

inspired ideal of a Christian church. All, from the preacher in the stand to the feeblest and most illiterate member in the pew, should have an "anointing that abideth and teacheth." Consequently much of the teaching would be unofficial, and what would be regarded as irregular; but as the "spirits of the prophets are subject to the prophets," and "obey them that have the rule," no collisions would occur. So also there is in this prophecy the New Testament idea of a Christian family; the parents, sons, daughters, and servants should all possess and employ the prophetic gift. Such an instance of a Christian family was found in the household of Philip the evangelist; he "had four daughters, and they all did prophesy" — they "spake unto men to edification, exhortation, and comfort."

The Duty Urged in the Text

"Despise not prophesying." This charge to a Christian church indicates that good people may be so poorly instructed with regard to duty and privilege as not only to be destitute of the gift under consideration, but even despise its exercise by others. Hence the text guards against this, and urges,

1. *The approval of prophesyings.* — The itinerant preacher may underrate the labors of the local preacher; the local preacher the labors of the exhorter; the exhorter may despise the more humble services of the class-leader, and all may feel mortification when the obscure servant-girl, under the inspiration of a glowing religious experience, and the mighty promptings of the prophetic Spirit, "speaks unto men to edification, exhortation, and comfort." And if obscure persons not officially recognized as teachers should be so filled with the spirit of prophecy that they go where openings are made for their humble labors it is not to be wondered at if some of the wise in the Church should take steps, to suppress the irregular-

ity. Nor is it strange that these humble Christian laborers who, as Jeremiah expresses it, "have the word in their hearts as a burning fire shut up in their bones, and are weary of forbearing," should find it a great trial of their charity to reconcile such steps with Christian character and a love of souls. Such occurrences prove that good men may be ignorant of the true prophetic gift and need the caution of the text. In thus despising prophesyings they may not criminate themselves, but certainly display much less acquaintance with the divine mind than God's ancient servant who, under like circumstances, said "would to God all the Lord's people were prophets, and that he would put his Spirit upon them." Not only are prophesyings to be approbated but,

2. *Attentively heard.* — It is a fearful mistake for any Christian to reach the conclusion that he no longer needs the instruction of those over him in the Lord, no matter how shallow may be their acquaintance with divine things. Though the Christian may have "an unction from the Holy One, and know all things," he may not neglect the divinely-appointed channels of religious knowledge. This would be to violate the order under consideration, and despise prophesyings. Nor is the obligation changed by the consideration that he may not admire nor enjoy the services of his religious teacher. "All are yours," says the apostle; "whether Paul, or Apollos, or Cephas," and it may be more necessary for the discipline needed, and for the culture of defective graces, to endure the services of an unappreciated Cephas than to enjoy the labors of the favorite Apollos. It is a sad day for them and the churches they serve, when regularly constituted teachers of righteousness conclude that the lowly of the church cannot serve as channels of communication from God to them, and, unlike the eloquent Apollos, refuse to sit at the feet of some Aquila and Priscilla and learn the "way of God more perfectly." Preachers, and all others, should "prove

all things and hold fast that which is good," no matter how humble the origin.

3. *Earnestly covet and perseveringly seek the desirable gift.* — As reference has already been made to the inspired order to "desire" and "covet" this gift, let the attention now be turned to the voice which comes from the families, neighbors, citizens, and fellow-mortals every-where calling for help. Amid this loud and universal cry for help it is painful to see the numbers who ought to be efficient workers *dull* and *dumb*; some willfully and others ignorantly deficient in the power to help. The word is not in "their hearts as fire shut up in their bones," impelling them forward, in the face of all opposition, to save their perishing fellows. The unconverted sit with them at their tables, work with them in their shops, deal with them in their business, and crowd against them in the highways, and they have no heart to use the golden opportunity to save them. They excuse themselves because they have no freedom in religious conversation with the unsaved; because they do not want to be meddlesome; they do not want to make disturbance; they do not want to be singular and have people shun them; they do not want to appear overrighteous; and they do not want to appear like specialists and disturb the quietude of many good people, and possibly produce schism. The text demands a deliverance from all these bonds and the acceptance of spiritual freedom and power that will hasten to save souls regardless of the frowns of wickedness and the sneers of formalism.

The Gospel provides that all shall have a deep insight into the word, and a tongue of fire to communicate the knowledge to others. The results that would follow the universal possession and exercise of this wonderful endowment are clearly pointed out. The apostle says, "ye may all prophesy one by one," and "if all prophesy and there come in one that believeth not" — that is, a common infidel — "or one unlearned" — that is, a heathen person — "he is convinced of all, he is judged of all; and thus are the secrets of his heart made manifest;" — that is, he is convicted of sin — "and so falling down upon his face he will worship God," — that is, get converted "and report that God is in you of a truth." I Cor. 14. 24-25. No pagan, no professed skeptic, no sinner of any character, unless, perhaps, it would be a religious formalist, who is more imperiled than the publican or harlot, can stand before such a Christian society.

O for a return of those times of Methodism when nearly all bearing the reproachful name were sanctified wholly, and endowed with an unction that was continually instructing, persuading, and leading the perishing to Christ!

XXVII
NURSING YOUNG CONVERTS

He exhorted them all, that with purpose of heart they would cleave unto the Lord. —Acts 11. 23.

DURING THE WINTERS many thousands of persons are brought into the churches, and the question of building them up in the faith is a problem of paramount importance with every faithful pastor and worthy official board. Nothing furnished upon the subject, either by the pulpit or religious press, will likely pass unnoticed by the men and women charged with this work and interested in the welfare of their respective societies.

In the Acts of the Apostles, 11. 23-25, there is a very instructive lesson upon this theme which may be studied with unusual interest and profit. It is narrated that after an extensive work of grace, reaching many Gentiles at Antioch, the Church at Jerusalem sent Barnabas to investigate the work, and, if genuine, organize and care for it. In the verses referred to it is stated that "when he came, and had seen the grace of God, he was glad, and exhorted them all that with purpose of heart they would cleave unto the Lord. For he was a good man, and full of the Holy Ghost and of faith; and much people was added unto the Lord. Then departed Barnabas to Tarsus, for to seek Saul." There are in this narrative, intended for the edification of the future Church an inspired example of building up young Christians, some suggestions of importance which will now be stated and briefly discussed.

A very significant fact in the work "after the revival," and one that cannot be too closely and prayerfully studied, is the character given to the nurse mentioned in the record. "He was a good man, and full of the Holy Ghost and of faith." He was a man from whom the "bad" in human nature had been eliminated and its place supplied with the Holy Spirit in his fullness of faith, love, peace, joy, long-suffering, gentleness, goodness, and the other graces. Hence he had no prejudices against the revival work because he did not lead it, or because it was brought about by some zealous laymen from Cyprus and Cyrene, or because it took place in an irregular way under the labors of unlicensed workers, or because it was among the Gentiles whom he had been educated, with his countrymen in general, to call "dogs." Like every other Spirit-baptized person he was pleased at "the grace of God," no matter among whom it might be displayed, nor by whom it might be introduced.

The Church has suffered immensely after revivals because she could not furnish nurses filled with the Spirit, and who could rise in their work above petty prejudices; but because some had come from low families and promised little, because others had been moved under great revival excitement and not been sufficiently considerate, because others had been led by traveling evangelists and not by regular pastors, and because of various other silly and insufficient reasons, thousands have been allowed to sicken and die who might, with proper care, have been saved to Christ and his Church. Full salvation furnishing its subjects with superior light, love and power, this narrative assures us, would have led to very different views, prompted to very different action, and produced very different results.

Another valuable hint, casting light upon the problem of nursing, comes from the pabulum with which Barnabas fed the young converts. "He exhorted them all, that with purpose of heart they would cleave unto the Lord." The Greek text is peculiarly significant. The definite article is employed before both the words rendered "purpose" and "heart;" and the word rendered "purpose" is a compound expressing a first or primary position or purpose. The word rendered "cleave unto" is another compound, and means to remain close to or near by. The whole phrase, therefore, could be literally rendered: He exhorted all, that with *the first purpose of the heart they should remain near by the Lord*. This literal rendering fully expanded makes Barnabas say to these young Christians: Whatever may be your purposes concerning business, domestic, social, and other interests, let the purpose to continue religious take precedence and rise above all others. And since you have had a struggle to submit yourselves to God, since you have had to stem the current of your nature to become Christian, let the purpose to remain Christian become the purpose of *the heart*; let the whole affectional nature become enlisted; continue to remain near your Lord, and look to him to so change the current of your affections that they will flow toward him, and duty then will become privilege and the Christian life a luxury.

It will be noticed that this exhortation calls the minds of the converts to their already properly-adjusted moral relations with God and their high privileges in Christ while these relations are maintained. Duty in the use of the means of grace and other Christian work is not made prominent, and is in striking contrast with the counsels of the modern class-leader, who exhorts the tempted and disheartened convert to "go on, be faithful, attend the class, and use all the means of grace." This is good advice, of course, if properly interpreted, but never used by those who possess the grace enjoyed by Barnabas, and use it wisely in counselling others. It conceals, or places in the back ground, grace and privilege, and brings into prominence and makes primary the use of means and duty; which soon become distasteful and are abandoned, as all observers know, unless the inner life be fed and take precedence of the outer.

It will be noticed that this exhortation of Barnabas contrasts sharply also with the counsel of those teachers of holiness who have wandered in the wilderness and had a Jordan crossing into Canaan— an experience much like their Red Sea passage or conversion, and who suppose that all others, young and old, faithful or unfaithful, must have the same. These speak to young converts of the necessity of new acts of submission, of deeper consecrations, and of awful interior crucifixions to reach a state of purity. This is not what a young convert needs. His submission is complete, his attitude toward God and man is right; and what he needs is encouragement to receive by simple faith a perfect deliverance from the inbeing of sin to which he is now entitled. Had ancient Israel passed into Canaan at Kadesh he would have crossed nothing but a geographical line. So young converts need no Jordan passage; only those who refuse holiness at the proper time and wander into the wilderness must cross a Jordan. Wesley, in his "Plain Account," states this clearly in the following question and answer: "But may we continue in peace and joy till we are perfect in love? Answer. Certainly we may, for the kingdom of God is not divided against itself. Therefore let not believers be discouraged from *rejoicing in the Lord always*."

Such a presentation of Christian privilege will dishearten no young convert; but to talk to them of a need of Jordan crossings and crucifixions which, in the nature of the case, they cannot feel, or to urge them to the use of the means of grace for the purpose of gradually developing the new life received at conversion, is to drive them back into the world, or to a tread-mill use of the means without any conscious advance in grace. The only true nursing of neophyte believers is clearly indicated in this record and other Scriptures which speak on the same subject.

Another important suggestion is found in the *manner* in which Barnabas exhorted the young converts. The narrator uses the Greek words *parekalei pantas— para with the accusative—* indicating that he placed himself among them all and at the side of each, and called upon them, from this position of oneness and sympathy with them, to embrace their privilege in the Gospel. He did not stand off in official dignity and give utterance to scriptural rules of holy living, but, in spite of early education and deep-seated prejudice, he identifies himself with these Gentile converts, and easily leads them forward to such an intimate acquaintance with Christ, and to the manifestation of such holiness of life, that "much people was added to the Lord," and Antioch made the center of Gentile Christianity.

If all who have charge of the spiritual interest of the churches had the grace which governed Barnabas, and used it with the same wisdom, they would care nothing for the manner in which, nor the persons by whom, the converts were added to the company of believers. They would be so interested in placing stars in the Redeemer's crown that they would gladly "to the weak become as weak," and become "all things to all, that by all means they might save some."

XXVII: Nursing Young Converts   **177**

The only other suggestion to be noticed at present is found in the call of Saul from Tarsus to assist in a work which had become too extensive for one pastor and his helpers. The lesson is, those churches which have gathered into their folds hundreds of young converts ought, by all means, to hunt up some Saul of Tarsus, or some Phœbe, a servant of the Church, to aid the pastor and local help in caring for the babes in Christ. The additional expense would be easily met by the converts themselves if so instructed, who, if not properly cared for, would spend many-fold more money at places of ruinous amusement and be lost entirely to the Church. Attention to this inspired hint by church authorities would greatly enrich the Church of God in money, in spirituality and in number.

Let this inspired method of treating young Christians be carefully studied by pastors and official boards; let them scrupulously practice the lessons learned, and the question, "How shall we entertain, interest and hold the young people of the Church?" will have a satisfactory solution. They will be abundantly satisfied with the fatness of God's house and drink from the river of his pleasure.

A supreme need of the Church at this hour is Spirit-baptized nurses, endued with heavenly wisdom, to care for her babes and bring up a stalwart race of Christians.

XXVIII
Successful Evangelism

Take heed unto thyself, and unto the doctrine; continue in them: for in doing this thou shalt both save thyself and them that hear thee. —I Tim. 4. 16.

THIS SCRIPTURE FURNISHES an inspired answer to a great number of very important questions frequently asked in this day. The faithful Sunday-school teacher is asking with solicitude, How shall I secure the awakening and conversion of my pupils? And here is the inspired answer: "Take heed unto thyself, and unto the doctrine; continue in them." The faithful class-leader is asking, How shall I lead the members of my class into deeper spiritual life? And he finds an answer in the same words. The true preacher is asking, What shall I do to build up my church in faith and holiness, and bring sinners to the cross? And a divine voice of authority says: "Take heed unto thyself, and unto the doctrine; continue in them: for in doing this thou shalt save thyself, and them that hear thee." The great popular question among the churches, How shall we reach the masses, as well as all other subordinate ones, finds a true answer in this Scripture. The answer consists of three parts, which we now notice:

1. *"Take heed unto thyself."* — The Greek word rendered "take heed" is compounded of *epi*, upon, and *echo* to seize; and the *epi* here is before a dative, and means *close upon*. Hence the compound word literally translated is, seize close upon, or take a top grip upon thyself. Hence the first great matter in effective religious labor is proper self-control, embracing right moral relations with God and man, and possessing a correct inward state of the heart. The Christian worker must be right himself; carefully separating himself from all that is displeasing to God, and accepting and practicing all that God approves. He must see that no self-seeking, no ambitious schemes, no unworthy measures, and no impure motives, enter into his plans and labors. He must see that he acts in the name and strength of his Lord, and not in his own, nor that of his Church; he must be sure to have a personal acquaintance with Jesus, to have a personal understanding with Jesus concerning the work in which he engages, and to be sure that he has a divine commission from Him to do the work in hand. He must see to it that his consecration is to God himself, as distinguished from the work of God. Many mistake a devotement to some line of work for devotion to God, and wonder why, in view of their deep interest in the work, they do not succeed better. The reason is they are idolators; they serve and worship the work rather than their Lord, and success would only deepen their idolatry and alienate them more and more from God. Hence He cannot give them prosperity, for it would hasten their ruin and mislead others. Here we find the cause of much of the sad failures we witness among the active and zealous laborers of the different churches. The

Lord cannot bless their work, for their moral relations with Him are not right; they do too much in their own strength, and are too much devoted to the work and too little to the Proprietor or Head of the work.

Another matter involved in the Christian laborer taking heed unto himself is the proper regulation of his own family, or those under his immediate care and control. One of the necessary qualifications of the deacons in the apostolic churches was that they rule their own children and houses well. It is a heavy discount on the labors of laymen or ministers when their own children are not under proper government; especially is this true of the preacher. A Christian family is a miniature church, and the Church of God takes its type and complexion from the families that compose it; and if the preacher who heads one of these families, and that one, too, which should be a model for all the rest, cannot or does not govern it, he is incompetent to regulate and govern the larger church made up of many families. Hence the apostle's question, "For if a man know not how to rule his own house, how shall he take care of the Church of God? Hence the first thing for a religious laborer, in any department of the work of God, is to see that his own heart is right, and that those under his immediate control be properly governed. Next thing to be done is,

2. *"Take heed unto the doctrine."* — The Greek word here rendered doctrine means teaching, and is so translated in the Revised Version. The order then is, Take a top hold upon the teaching, embracing both the *matter* and the *manner*. Let the matter be the word — the word of God. Paul says: "Preach the word;" not a mixture of the word and something else, but the pure word. Too much of what passes, these days, for preaching is nothing more or less than essays or discourses on history, philosophy, politics, and current events, with a little scriptural mixture to make them

pass for sermons. And much of that which is really scriptural, so far as the subjects and truths discussed are concerned, is so dressed, and presented in such a style, that nothing is noticed but the homiletics, the language, the figures the voice and movements of the reader or speaker. Such preaching moves no sinner to repentance; nor does it lead any believer into greater depths of spiritual life. There is no promise made to such religious exercises except, "Verily I say unto you. They have their reward."

The promise is to a very different kind of preaching, "Go ye therefore," says Jesus, "and teach all nations, baptizing them in the name of the Father, and of the Son, and of the Holy Ghost; *teaching them to observe all things whatsoever I have commanded you*: and lo, I am with you alway, even unto the end of the world." This is the teaching which Jesus accompanies and applies to the hearts of those who hear, and which bears fruit to the glory of God. Hence those evangelists, pastors, and teachers, who succeed in soul-saving, preach and teach the simple truths of the Gospel without any admixture, constantly holding up Jesus and his salvation. However wide the range the regular pastor, who is a soul-winner, feels he must take in his pulpit ministrations, he is very chary as to what he puts into his sermons. He finds in the Bible— what every other Spirit-illuminated teacher of sacred truth finds— more than enough for the widest range proper for the pulpit, and is not driven to magazine literature or the records of the daily newspapers for subjects and illustrations. He knows the more he adheres to the Bible the more he finds in it, the more interesting it becomes to himself, and the more interesting does he make it to others. But such is, and ever has been, the tendency to wander away from simple scriptural truth to what the apostle calls "oppositions of science falsely so called," that the preacher or teacher of righteousness must carefully observe the counsel of the text, or the wily enemy will soon interject foreign matter enough to cancel the soul-winning power of Gospel themes.

Another matter involved in taking heed to the doctrine is the *manner* of teaching. Christian workers should be so filled with the Spirit as to be intensely in earnest to save the people and build up the kingdom of Christ on earth. This would put vigor into their movements, true eloquence into their utterances, and true zeal into all their work. The enthusiasm which ambition to build up a cause awakens, the animation which large audiences will produce, and the eloquence which culture can furnish, may organize and build up religious clubs, but not Christian churches; they may make popular religious teachers, but will ruin their souls and the souls of those whom they lead. Such zeal and earnestness are mere imitations of the genuine unction, and those who knowingly use them in place of the true anointing incur the divine frown. It was a capital offense, punished by excision from the people of God under the Levitical code, to imitate the holy anointing oil; and it was the same, and punished in the same way, to compound the holy perfume for the mere purpose of perfumery, or "to smell thereto," as put in inspired verbiage. These Old Testament types indicate the criminality, under the Gospel dispensation, of using any imitation of the Spirit's anointing, and of framing and intonating prayers merely for the ears of others. Whoever dare do these things must suffer excision from the true, spiritual Israel. Hence the great importance of having a top grip upon the manner of all religious exercises, not only for personal safety and salvation, but for the salvation of others. Another vital matter is to,

3. *"Continue in them."* — The Greek word, *epimaneo*, here translated "continue," means to remain upon, and conveys the idea that, the Christian toiler having taken an upper grasp upon himself and his teaching, he should

remain master, and keep them under. This assumes that watchfulness and care are necessary, and without them the self-life and unprofitable discourse will assert themselves, take control of the laborer, and put him under. This is to-day, and has been in the past, the sad condition of many religious toilers. This failure to "continue in them" is an explanation of the fitful and spasmodic religious life of so many, and the fitful nature of revivals in general.

Church life has its beginnings, its continuance, its ebbings and flowings like individual religious life. When the sinner is aroused to notice his exposure he becomes alarmed and calls for mercy, finds pardon, and rejoices in his deliverance from guilt and misery. Before long, from a want of watchfulness and prayer, the self-life and world-liness may creep into the heart and take supremacy; then the happy convert goes under and becomes miserable, and in this condition he remains until the Holy Spirit arouses him again. So it is with church life and the revival spirit. Churches move along in formality and spiritual inaction till the preacher, or some of the members, or both, become alarmed, and get between the porch and the altar and cry unto God till he sends them times of refreshing. Then the preacher and members are made happy and rejoice together; and the preacher becomes a real apostle among the people; he is cajoled, and flattered, and invited to a participation in every thing which the membership and people think will make him happy. Whatever may be the craze at the time the preacher must share in the enjoyment which it can give; if it be croquet, he must enjoy a game with them; if euchre, he is pressed into it; if it be to travel abroad for sight-seeing, he must be the central figure of the party; any thing, now, to lion-ize and make him happy.

This is a trial season with the preacher; it is passing with his Lord through that crucial period when the people, delighted to frenzy, would take him by force and make a king. Many, however, do not see the peril, and fail to imitate their Master, who constrained the disciples to depart, sent the people away, and hastened to the mountain for prayer. Thus the preacher is led away "by little and little," unwittingly to himself, and unintentionally by the brethren, until his spiritual life has severely suffered, and the revival fires have died out in the church.

Besides this, since the revival has increased the membership, and some of the cultured of the neighborhood have joined the society, the church building must be repaired and put in good order. At this work they go, and all, as they ought, become interested and give their time and money to the work. The prayer-meetings and other services must be moved into a borrowed church, or rented hall, and some do not care to go to these new places of worship; others are tired, and, as they have been giving their labors and means to the repairs, they may be excused from the more spiritual work, and soon formalism has the supremacy. Some debt has been contracted for the repairs, and formalism soon suggests fairs, festivals, bazars, and so on, as the best method of meeting the liability. Very soon, then, a few written essays or sermons on Darwinism, Romanism, current events, and popular specialties, announce the absence of all revival power. In this condition the church will drag along again until God in mercy sounds another alarm, and the same thing is substantially repeated, all because of shameful neglect to "continue in them," and thereby practice the counsel of the text.

Revival fire is retained in the church just as it is obtained. Spiritual life in the individual is obtained by the utter abandonment of sin and the acceptance of Christ as a personal Saviour; and it is retained by the individual in constant self-abnegation, and implicit obedience to all the divine requirements, by walking in a way as narrow as the gate is strait. So the same deep humiliation and earnest looking to God which awakened the revival spirit must be cherished and preserved, to secure the continuance of awakenings, of conversions, and of spiritual growth. This continual earnestness and zeal in Christian labor are necessary to the continuance of the divine commission to save others. The Saviour said to his disciples, "As my Father hath sent me, even so send I you;" using the present tense, and indicating that the sending is, like the spiritual life, momentary, and perpetuated upon the condition of continuous loyalty. Hence the apostle in the text makes perseverance in self-control and true scriptural teaching necessary to personal salvation and success in general evangelism.

Here, then, we have the secret of success in Christian work. It is presented in the verbiage of our text: "Take heed unto thyself, and unto the doctrine; continue in them: for in doing this thou shalt both save thyself, and them that hear thee." It is a secret which every religious toiler may learn and use in his labor; and, if he will learn and practice it, he cannot fail. God spake these words through the apostle; and the Christian worker who fails in saving others that hear him, or habitually hear him, as the tense of the Greek verb indicates, should be profoundly moved by this inspired statement, and prayerfully inquire for the cause of his fruitless toil.

XXIX
THE EAST JORDANIC REST

Bring us not over Jordan. —Num. 32. 5.
Be sure your sin will find you out. —Num. 32. 23.

SINCE THE JORDAN PASSAGE INTO Canaan, according to the apostle, is a historic symbol of the believer's transition from a state of partial to a state of entire sanctification, the settlement and rest of the two and one half tribes on the east of Jordan must have a correspondence in actual religious life. Nine and one half tribes found their homes and rest on the west side of Jordan and in the promised land; the remaining two and one half found their homes and rest on the opposite side, and without the Jordan passage.

Perhaps, as a matter of fact, taking all of God's children in all the churches, about two and one half in every twelve find a true soul-rest without any well-defined passage from a weak and vacillating faith to full assurance of faith; but the great body of perfected believers are distinctly conscious of such transition. The former, of course, from the facts of their experience would question the ne-

cessity of "a second work," and would view their satisfactory and perfected experience as a development of
their converted state. All such persons should prayerfully
study two facts connected with the historic symbol of their
state, or the settlement of the two and one half tribes in
the kingdom of Og and Sihon.

1. *The original promise to Abraham, and the divine
arrangement for his posterity, did not contemplate the
settlement of any one outside of Canaan.—* This was
first suggested to Moses by the children of Reuben and
Gad, who were heavy cattle owners and who had discovered that these lands would afford pasturage for
their immense herds. The narrative is found in Num.
32. 1-33, and to it the reader is requested to turn and
examine. He will find, when the matter was first mentioned to Moses, that he stoutly opposed the measure
and sharply rebuked the applicants. He charges them
with rebellion against God, and a wicked imitation of
their rebellious fathers. But they proposed to him that,
if he would grant their request, they would prepare
folds for their cattle and fenced cities for their children, and there they would leave them and go before
their brethren across the Jordan, and fight with them
until they were peacefully settled in the promised land.
This struck Moses favorably and he consented to the
proposition, but not without most solemnly impress-
ing them with the sacredness of their covenant and
the awful consequences of its violation. In verse 23 he
assures them that a fearful retribution awaited a failure to meet this engagement. "But if ye will not do so,
behold, ye have sinned against the Lord: and be sure
your sin will find you out."

It will be seen from these facts that the settlement of
these tribes east of Jordan was not contemplated in God's
benevolent arrangements for them. It was a transaction
between them and Moses, and although God does not

seem to have objected, yet he never spoke of their possessions as an inheritance which he had given them, but as
the land which Moses gave them. The possessions of the
other tribes in Canaan are ever spoken of as the inheritance which the Lord their God gave them. He gave all
the tribes *rest*, but Moses gave the Reubenites, the Gadites,
and the half-tribes of Manassah, their *lands*.

Thus those believers who have found a satisfactory rest
to their souls, without a definite passage into the entirely
sanctified state, have an exceptional and not a general
experience. It is an experience not contemplated in the
gracious economy, is abnormal, and produced by some
human device which has beclouded the Spirit's operations and confounded his justifying and adopting love
with his purifying and empowering work. When the
Spirit's teachings and leadings are not obscured by prejudices, philosophizings, and false theories, penitents are
led to a joyful acceptance of Christ as a Saviour, and afterward as consciously receive the gift of the Holy Ghost.
This was true of the converts in the apostolic churches,
and has been true of believers ever since, where the Spirit
has not been obstructed in his leadings.

2. *Another fact to be carefully studied is, that the three
tribes scrupulously kept their engagement with Moses.* —
When the time came to lead the people across the Jordan
Joshua notified these tribes, and they promptly rushed to
the front, forty thousand strong; and, fully equipped for
battle, they marched before their brethren on to the plains
of Jericho.

For some seven years, according to the received chro-
nology, these warriors remained in Canaan, assisting in
subduing the country and establishing the tribes in their
homes. At the close of this period Joshua sent them away
to their own possessions, complimenting them for their
fidelity and valor, and with "much riches, very much
cattle, with silver, and with gold, and with very much

raiment." When they recrossed the Jordan to the land of Gilead they constructed a magnificent altar, which their brethren interpreted to mean either idolatry or civil independence. But to the embassy sent to inquire into the matter they declared that they intended it as a link of union to bind them and their children to the national religion and government. They did not dare to relinquish their claim upon the promised land and their interest in the Abrahamic promise. See this very interesting history in full as it is given in Josh. 22. 1-29.

The lesson is this: Those believers who have found rest without a Jordan passage, or without the definite work of entire sanctification, have found it upon a complete, unreserved, and eternal surrender of themselves to God. They have renounced every thing opposed to entire purity, and have consecrated their time, talents, influence, and every thing that appertains to them, to the cause and glory of God. This involves, of course, the work of helping their brethren, who have not found complete rest in their justified relation, to make a crossing into the entirely-sanctified state. Those who have found rest should, like the two and one half tribes, rush to the front of their brethren who have not found rest and aid them in its pursuit, or lead them from a partial to an entirely sanctified state. The historic type assures to such a course a rich reward, and the opposite course a fearful reckoning. It is an alarming fact, painful to record, that some of those ministers and laymen who profess to have found all their souls desired without the specific work of entire sanctification, and who have refused support to measures looking to such a work for unsatisfied believers, have left the Church in disgrace; and others, pursuing a similar course, are getting into trouble, losing their influence and going into entire eclipse. "But if ye will not do so, behold, ye have sinned against the Lord: and be sure your sin will find you out."

Dear brethren, if you have found your rest without the definite experience of entire purity, you dare not neglect your brethren who have not found it, but you must lead them forward until they hear the Spirit, "speak the second time. Be clean."

Nor can you afford to dissolve your connection with this Wesleyan and scriptural doctrine and experience. Your own interests and the interests of your children after you demand that you, like the two and one half tribes, build an altar upon this doctrine and the proper movements to spread it, and thereby perpetuate your connection with it.

XXX
ACTING IN THE NAME OF JESUS

Do all in the name of the Lord Jesus. —Col. 3. 11.

TO ACT IN THE NAME of another is common in the intercourse of man with man. The salesmen of business houses barter and sell in the name of the firms which they represent. The employés of banking institutions loan and discount in the name of these corporations. Government officials form alliances, make treaties, and do other public business in the name of the governments which they serve.

But it must be particularly noted that the exercise of these prerogatives supposes previous transactions by which these agents have been taken into the confidence of their respective principals. To act in the name of another without a mutual understanding and agreement is a fraud, and punishable as a crime. And, after such agreement, to betray the confidence reposed and use the money or name of principals for personal advantage, or in any way not stipulated, is taking criminal advantage of a position, and is a high misdemeanor.

Apply these facts to the subject in hand, and it will be

seen that to act in the name of the Lord Jesus involves some important matters too generally over- looked even by earnest Christians.

1. *Those who truly act in the name of Jesus have been taken into his confidence.* — They have made an unconditional surrender to God, renounced self and all other masters and principals, and accepted Christ as their only Lord and Saviour. Their faith has apprehended the fact that they have been taken into his confidence, and are hereafter, during their loyalty, authorized to act in his name. Without such an antecedent fact or transaction, to act in the name of Jesus is a fraud. Any person may use the name of some moneyed celebrity for the purpose of getting credit, or some other personal advantage; but, without a mutual understanding, such use is criminal conduct.

Now, it is to be feared that there are thousands who do not intend to be dishonest, and who are trying to do Christian work in the name of the Lord Jesus, that have never been taken into this divine confidence and fellowship; and their sad failures are painful evidences of their error. They wonder why they do not succeed as well, and even better, than their brethren whose native talents are so much less. They do not suspect that their moral relations are wrong, and that they unwittingly use the name of Jesus like rogues who place upon their paper the forged names of others. They have not met the conditions of a divine commission.

2. *Those who truly act in the name of Jesus feel intrusted with immense interests.* — The agents of merchant princes and railway kings are not employed with trifles. The one does not deal in the petty quantities of small retailers, nor is the other found contracting for a few dozens of toy locomotives and cars. Such bartering would let down the honor and dignity of their employers. So those who really act in the name of Jesus are not decoyed into useless

and unimportant exercises. They feel charged with the incalculably important work of saving themselves and those around them. Hence they subordinate all secular duties to this end, and thus invest the little matters of every-day life with an importance which strips them of dullness and insipidity. Necessary secular toil becomes the tent-making essential to support the business of soul-saving— an enterprise in the presence of which railroad projects, national improvements, and international schemes dwindle into comparative insignificance.

In the face of this fact it is painful to note that many bearing the name of Christ, and numbered among Christian workers, ask for little in their prayers and expect less in their labors. It is distressing to see how readily they descend from their lofty mission to busy themselves with dangerous trifles, and how readily they yield to the foolish customs of the world, the clamors of sensual pleasure and the demands of vain ambitions. All this involves an appalling misapprehension of the Christian's high vocation.

3. *Those who truly act in the name of Jesus carry a truly sublime and heavenly bearing.*— Government officials of correct moral sentiments dress and converse and move with becoming dignity. Should they descend to the appearance of common servants or common sensualists they would debase themselves and dishonor their governments. So, those who scripturally do all in the name of the Lord Jesus move with an air which becomes the Gospel of Christ. With a mien allied to the heavenly, they pity and love enemies; they wash, with unaffected humility, the disciples' feet; they sympathize with the unfortunate and lowly; they prefer the honor of others to their own, and, in every way, remind observers of the lowly Nazarene.

It is therefore, a monstrous impertinence for persons assuming the name of Christian to have little or no com-

passion on the erring, to have little or no love for the out-
casts of society, to eagerly seek their own honor and happiness to the neglect of others', or in other ways to mis-
represent the Lord whose name they assume to bear. And,
if painful facts did not compel the belief, it would be difficult to allow that there could be a blindness which would
use this sacred name to gain the favor of good people, to
reach place and position, to obtain support and patronage, and to secure personal aggrandizement in other
ways.

4. *Those who truly act in the name of Jesus are partakers
of his nature.* — Commercial travelers carry with them
specimens of the goods produced by the manufacturing
establishments which they represent. This is done that
buyers may be induced to purchase by placing before
them the different kinds and qualities of the goods which
they hold on the market. So, while Christians are ordered
to "go, work," they are also commanded to "tarry" until
purified and empowered, and until they can show forth
in their spirit and movements the lovely graces of the
Saviour whom they represent. True believers present true
specimens of the Spirit's work upon the human heart, and
they become the "saved saviours" of others. Of his fullness have we all received, and grace for grace." "As he is,
so are we in this world." What a wonder of grace!

Few modern religious workers make this high ideal such
a realized experience as to say with Paul, "Be ye followers of me, even as I also am of Christ;" and, again, "Brethren, be followers together of me, and mark them which
walk so as you have us for an ensample." Paul felt bound,
by his original commission, to be a witness, and point to
himself as a *fac-simile* [*sic*] of his Lord. And who among
Christian workers has a right to fall below this, while before every believer there stands written "Let this mind be
in you, which was also in Christ Jesus?" Will the sickly
sentimentalism of the modern Church, which has nearly

suppressed testimony, justify silence upon the samples of grace which true Christians are supposed to carry with them in their experience and life? Nay, but it increases the obligation to obtain a Christ-like nature and demeanor and to declare their source.

5. *Those who truly act in the name of Jesus have an assurance of success in the work.* — The agents of railroad kings would not think of failure in the construction of a few miles of railway which they may be commissioned to build. These names represent too much capital, and can command too much of every thing necessary to the enterprise, to allow any doubt of success. So, to true faith, "the Name high over all" represents resources too immense to allow doubt of success in any work to which there is a clear divine call. In the truest use of this name no religious enterprise is attempted without a divine commission; and within this limit almightiness is pledged for victory, and faith apprehends this fact and inspires assurance. Hence, those who have been admitted to the divine confidence and fellowship feel that

"To doubt would be disloyalty,
    To falter would be sin."

In the light of all these facts Christendom certainly presents a sad spectacle. It is doubtful whether more than one in ten of all who claim to be followers of Christ use his name in this highest and best sense, and the great body in any true sense whatever. Many use the name, perhaps, in a true sense, but not in the highest and best sense. Some great and good capitalists keep in their employ agents whose weakness and want of qualifications are great trials to their employers, and merit dismissal; but they are retained through simple benevolence. So, the compassionate Saviour keeps among his servants many very weak and unworthy ones who frequently doubt and otherwise dishonor him. They damage the

Master's business, and yet through mercy they are retained, with a continued call to a better and more satisfactory experience and life.

Reader, have *you* ever been formally taken into the confidence and fellowship of your Lord, or do you use his name without any definite covenant between you and him? And if you have been truly enrolled with his servants do you use his name with fidelity, and do you condescend to nothing dishonoring to your Lord who hath called you to his kingdom and glory?

XXXI
An Analysis of the Spirit's Work in the Heart

Now he which stablisheth us with you in Christ, and hath anointed us, is God; who hath also sealed us, and given the earnest of the Spirit in our hearts. —2 Cor. 1. 21, 22 .

IN THIS REMARKABLE STATEMENT of the apostle he evidently has his eye upon the subjective work of the Spirit in the believer's heart, and by this analysis brings to view its elements, or different parts. First in Christ, then established in him, then anointed in this established union, then sealed in this established and anointed union, and, lastly, possessed of the earnest of the Spirit. He is careful to note, also, that this gracious work is the heritage of all Christians. "He which stablisheth us"— apostles— "with you"— the laity— "and hath anointed us, is God." Both the ministry and membership have equal claims upon this grace, and both are equally under obligation to seek it, and are equally benefited by its possession. Let us study these parts separately.

1. *In Christ.* — The expressions, "In Christ," "in Christ Jesus," "in the Lord," and similar wordings, are favorites with the apostle Paul to express the gracious state, and are frequently met with in reading his epistles. By them he means such a union with Christ as he symbolizes by the wild olive branches grafted into the tame; and this is such a living connection as causes the succulence of the trunk to flow freely into the grafts, producing growth and fruitfulness. So, to be "in Christ" is such a vital union with him that all Christly qualities live and grow in the believer.

As it is necessary, in forming this connection between the grafts and the trunk, that the grafter separate the scions from the parent trees, and carefully pare each one separately so that bark fits to bark, pore to pore, and fiber to fiber, so the penitent seeker of salvation must submit to a complete separation from sinners; he must place himself passive in the hands of the Holy Spirit, consenting to all the excision necessary for insertion into Christ Jesus. Birth in a Christian family, education in a Christian school, and training in a Christian Church, and all the discipline possible by religious teachers, cannot form this vital union. Nothing short of a specific and definite act of the Holy Ghost performed upon the heart, in response to the prayer of faith, can place the soul "in Christ Jesus" and produce a truly gracious state.

2. *Established in Christ* — It is one thing to be in Christ and quite another to be established in him. Many come into Christ by regenerating grace and soon lapse back into sin. Many believers come into a more blessed and intimate union with him by the work of entire sanctification, and lose and recover this grace a few times before they become established. His biographer states that the sainted Fletcher lost the experience of perfect love three or four times before he was rooted and grounded in it. There is, however, provision made to settle and fix believers in their walk with

God; not by the slow process of repeated acts of devotion, forming what is known as religious habits, but by an establishment which is as supernatural as the ingrafting into Christ, and is produced by the same Spirit. He which stablisheth us with you in Christ, *is God.*" Hence it is a supernatural rooting and grounding of which the apostle here speaks.

This establishment must not be interpreted to mean such a fixity in this gracious state as excludes the possibility of falling, but such a restful and happy union with Jesus that the believer feels that he *will not fall*, but not that he *cannot fall*. Paul had the assurance that he should continue through his future to possess "the fullness of the blessing of the Gospel," yet he felt the necessity of keeping under his body— the *soma*, or animal man— lest after having preached to others he himself might be a castaway. It must be noted, too, that this steadfastness in a gracious state is not on a dead level of experience, but in a love which "follows on to know the Lord," and aims to become more and more Christ-like and efficient in religious work. It is a fixity in an onward and upward movement in the divine life; "forgetting those things which are behind, and reaching forth unto those things which are before, it presses toward the mark."

Inasmuch as this rooting and grounding in love is a divine work it must be sought as definitely as the inward cleansing itself. The believer should go to God and covenant with him for his establishing and keeping power. He should fix it in his mind that he must never prove disloyal, but go to his knees with all his heart and ask God to remove him out of the world, rather than he shall deny his Lord and lose this grace. He will find, upon doing this in good faith, that it will be an effective spur to fidelity and an end of wavering and vacillation. Another part of this work to notice is,

3. *Anointed in this established union.* — The word

"anointed" is an Old Testament word brought over into the New to convey an important thought. To see its full significance we must go back to the ancient symbol, and look at its meaning and use under the Levitical ceremonial. In Ex. 30 there is a full account of the compounding of the holy anointing oil and the laws that regulated its use. It was made of certain sweet spices and olive oil, carefully prepared by the art of the apothecary, and was an expressive symbol of the gentle, tender, loving, yet penetrating energy of the Holy Spirit. It was poured upon kings at their inauguration and upon priests at their installation, signifying the impartation of supernatural endowments for the functions of their respective offices. The laws governing its use forbid its application to a stranger, or one not belonging to the Abrahamic family; they forbid its application to "man's flesh," the symbol of the carnal principle; and they forbid compounding any like it, or using any but the genuine article divinely prepared, and this only upon suitable subjects.

An application of these facts to the spiritualities of the New Testament will disclose the full meaning of the word. To be anointed, then, is to have the Holy Spirit poured upon us, giving a divine insight into the Scriptures, a supernatural freedom and readiness in communicating truth, and a divine afflatus or breath to accompany our utterances to the hearts of those who hear. This anointing can come on no alien, but only on such as are truly born of God and belong to the spiritual Israel. It can come on none who may have ambitious schemes to serve, nor upon any retaining the carnal principle divinely symbolized by "man's flesh." It can come on none who are willing to use their natural oratory, or acquired elocution, or their native zeal, or the enthusiasm excited by great assemblies, or the animation awakened by the hope of success, or any thing else as substitutes for the ardor, energy, and zeal of the Holy Spirit. Not until the believer feels that he can do no more preaching, or class-leading, or Sunday-school teaching, or any other Christian work without the anointing, can it come upon him. The self-life must be crucified, self-seeking and all perverse measures must be abandoned, and inward purity must take place, before this divine endowment can be realized and used. Many are pleading and waiting for the anointing, and wondering why they do not receive it, while they are at a vast moral distance from the point where it is possible for it to take place. They are attempting the impossible task of persuading God to pour holy oil on "man's flesh." Another part is,

4. *Sealed with the Holy Spirit of promise.*— Sealing is a stamp placed upon something as a proprietary mark, or to give it official recognition. Placed upon paper containing an article of agreement or a transfer of property, it makes the instrument binding, and gives it recognition in the courts. Placed by legal authority upon a measure, it is an official attestation that the measure is correct; placed upon a weight, it makes it legally exact; and any thing measured or weighed by these articles is a legal tender of the things so weighed and measured.

When God puts his seal upon the believer's heart he marks him as belonging to his "peculiar people;" he declares that the covenant between them is ratified and accepted in the court above; he declares that such believer contains, for one of his capacity, the right measure of grace and right moral weight in his family, church, and community. He may have but little compared with others of much greater natural endowments, and may seem very defective to his fellows, yet he is perfectly pleasing to Him who judges righteous judgment, and he has continually answered to his consciousness the prayer,

"I want the witness, Lord,
That all I do is right."

It is no humiliation to him that he seems to others "less than the least of all saints," and that he is himself conscious of littleness. He has no ambition but to please his Lord and to be numbered among the little ones by and through whom God carries on the evangelization of the world. As the great part of the business which hums and buzzes in commercial circles is carried on by the little weights and measures, so the soul-saving enterprises of Christendom are moved by the average preachers and common laymen, or by those "peculiar people" who can be sent anywhere and used at all times. One more part of this work remains to be noticed:

5. *The earnest of the Spirit in the heart.*— By this the apostle may mean that ardent, intent, and zealous religious state manifested by those who are "dead indeed unto sin, but alive unto God." Such persons are animated in their religious exercises, eager and warm in their Christian work, and in this sense have the earnest of the Spirit. He may mean, also, that installment of heavenly blessedness which God gives to those whom he seals as his own.

The earnest money among men is an advanced payment binding the contract, and a guarantee that the balance pledged is forthcoming, and to be the same currency or coin as that given in hand. So our gracious God deigns to enter into covenant with us, to seal the contract with the Spirit, and to import and lodge in the treasury of the heart as much of heaven as we can receive. It is a clear revelation to the consciousness of union with Jesus, of union established, of established union anointed, and anointed union sealed with the Spirit. Such a revelation is as much of the celestial as is possible and profitable while in the body.

No doubt this subjective work of the Spirit exists in all its entirety in dim outline upon every truly regenerated heart, but requires pentecostal fire to bring these outlines into bold relief. The young convert is very happy in the effects of this work upon his sensibilities, but has no ideas of anointing, sealing, and other parts of the work done feebly upon the heart. A discovery of spiritual feebleness, of the need of entire purification, or deliverance from the birth sin, and an application to the Sanctifier, are necessary to bring these matters to the soul's consciousness. The apostle is careful to keep before the reader, too, that this is not the product of culture and discipline, but a post-conversion work of the Spirit. "Now he which stablisheth us with you in Christ, and hath anointed us, is God; who hath also sealed us, and given us the earnest of the Spirit in our hearts."

In seeking a realization of this gracious work the believer should not attempt, as many do, to investigate and comprehend its nature, but, in utter self-abnegation, accept the merciful tender, count it his from that moment onward, and keep the eye on the Christ already received, till the Holy Spirit brings clearly to the consciousness the fact that "the great transaction is done." He should act in this matter as he would if a wealthy father would hand him a title deed for an immense tract of valuable land which he never saw. He would thankfully accept the deed and count the land his, and examine its locality, its quality, and its boundaries at his leisure. So, if we were wise in the things of God, we would take at once what he offers us, count them ours, and investigate them afterward, when we shall have all of time and eternity to estimate the greatness of the gifts.

To enjoy this grace fully, and use it efficiently, the believer must stand out prominently before the Church and world, both by testimony and life, as a person in Christ, as a person established in Christ, as an anointed person, as one sealed with the Holy Spirit, and as one filled with the fullness of God. Any shrinking from this position will bring mist and dimness upon the spiritual vision.

XXXII
QUALIFICATION OF CHURCH OFFICIALS

Wherefore, brethren, look ye out among you seven men of honest report, full of the Holy Ghost and wisdom, whom we may appoint over this business. —Acts 6. 3.

THE BUSINESS MENTIONED HERE was the distribution of the charities of the Church among her beneficiary widows. It seems from the record that the apostles had appointed certain persons to this work, but they had failed to render satisfaction to the Grecian membership. To obviate this difficulty the apostles fell upon the wise plan of allowing the multitude of the disciples to select from their number and nominate persons for this work, and they would appoint them; and thereby all would share the responsibility of any failure or dissatisfaction that might arise. They were ordered to choose men of "honest report," "full of the Holy Ghost and wisdom," and thus the qualifications of church officials in all after ages have been clearly defined. They were to be of—

1. *Honest Report.* — As these officials were to be chosen

from among the number of the disciples the reputation demanded was for both spirituality and good morals. Without a good reputation for truth and honesty the members of the Church would not feel safe to intrust them with funds given for distribution among the needy. And at this date it had already appeared, in the case of Ananias and Sapphira, that there were persons in the Pentecostal Church who could not be trusted in every respect. Whatever grace had done for them they were not scrupulously careful in the nice distinctions between certain forms of truth and falsehood, honesty and dishonesty, and were, therefore, not suited to responsible positions in the Church of God. Hence the ethical notions and practices of the men selected were to be carefully examined. Moreover, as their business would bring them in contact with the aged, the poor, the sick, and the suffering, they needed spiritual qualifications to administer religious instruction and comfort. Hence their piety, as well as their ethics, had to be taken into consideration.

The modern Church has been too careless in filling her offices. She has appointed to Sabbath-school work, to the post of trustees, and other responsible positions, persons who have not possessed these necessary qualifications. There are characters found among almost all bodies of professed believers who seem to have a good degree of spirituality, but who cannot be trusted with the funds of the Church, and who cannot be relied upon in any financial engagement which they may make. While they seem to be honest and sincere, they have no discretion in making such engagements, and even less in their efforts to meet them. They are religious enigmas to their brethren, and are clearly ineligible to any of the offices of the Church.

Then there are persons inside and outside of the Church who possess a high degree of moral honesty, and could be trusted with any of the Church's secularities, but they are destitute of the sanctity which such positions demand. The Church of late days has, nevertheless, appointed such disqualified persons to her offices, and apologized for it by the specious argument that she reaps the benefit of their good morals and financial support, and frequently leads them, by these conciliatory measures, to true repentance and faith in Christ. But granting this happy issue in many cases, is it clear that the cause is more helped than injured by such a policy? Does the example of Christ and the apostles justify the course? Paul could not tolerate the testimonial and aid of the damsel possessed with the spirit of divination, who declared, "These men are the servants of the most high God, which show unto us the way of salvation." At the risk of a general disturbance, of being thrust into a Philippian dungeon and of losing his life, he ordered this to be stopped. He courted no such aid. When the Saviour had an opportunity, by a little compromise, of affiliating with himself and the little company of his humble disciples a young governor of unimpeachable character, of high social position and influence, and of great wealth, he refused to do it upon any other terms than an unconditional and irreversible surrender of the entire man and all his money. How different the policy of the modern Church, and how weak is she as a necessary sequence! Another qualification named is—

2. *Full of the Holy Ghost.* — Ordinary sanctity was not enough. The apostles required that the nominees should possess the *fullness* of the Holy Ghost. Anything short of this fullness rendered a disciple ineligible to the office of a distributor of the churches' benefactions. Hence weak believers or persons of low spirituality could not be chosen to this work. And the propriety of this will appear when we remember that spiritual feebleness is not a necessity with any one. While it may be a necessity for a short season, and hence innocent to be a weak Christian,

it is a great shame and sin to *remain* weak, since God has provided something better, and ordered believers to accept it. He has ordered them to be "strong in the Lord," and no one can therefore innocently remain weak. Hence a believer who chooses to remain weak in the face of these provisions and this order, which make the fullness of the Holy Ghost a gift receivable now, is unworthy of official position in the Church of God.

This fullness of the Spirit, which involves a divine insight into the Scriptures and a readiness and liberty in using inspired truth, was to qualify these officials to prophesy in connection with the exercise of their official functions. The New Testament idea of a church is that all its members, from the preacher, the official head, down to the humblest member, shall have this divine illumination and freedom in utterance, so that all may "speak unto men to edification, exhortation and comfort" in their several spheres. Especially, then, should officials have this endowment.

This fullness was necessary also to give that anointing, or mysterious divine afflatus and breath, which is indispensable to carry religious truth to the understanding and heart. This is God speaking in the utterances of anointed persons, so that those addressed feel that God speaks. It is the particular endowment which the Saviour received at his baptism, and which he offers to all his followers so that they may be able, as was he, to preach the Gospel to the poor and to heal the broken hearted. Without this the letter which "killeth" only mocks the poor, and opens afresh the wounds of sorrowing hearts. Hence the hardness apparent in all communities where there has been much Bible teaching and pulpit labor done in a mere official and perfunctory manner. Hence, also, the shrinking of deeply-afflicted persons from pastors and religious teachers who desire to heal the wounds, but who, for the want of this unction, only deepen the sorrow. There is no divine and healing balm in the word as used by such persons, and no soft almighty hand is placed beneath by gospel promises uttered without the fullness of the Holy Ghost. Hence the necessity of all religious teachers, and especially church officials, being filled with the Spirit. Another qualification named is—

3. *Full of wisdom.*— Wisdom is the right use or exercise of knowledge, and is seen in the choice of laudable ends and the selection of the best means to accomplish them. The text implies, and observation confirms it, that persons may be filled with the Spirit and not have any natural or gracious aptitude for certain work. The discretion of the Church is, therefore, to be carefully exercised in the selection of her official workers.

Wisdom may be natural or gracious, and it is indifferent which be used provided it be such as can properly manage the work of God. Many have a large share of this quality by native endowment, and they are successful in all their undertakings. They appear to understand themselves, and attempt nothing above their ability to manage; they select the right thing, commence at the right time, prosecute in the right way, and achieve their purposes. This wisdom, brought under the power of grace, makes them eminently successful in working for the cause of Christ. Others seem greatly destitute of this endowment; they are sure to select some business or enterprise for which they have no aptitude, commence at an inopportune time, prosecute in a wrong way and utterly fail. These persons are failures in whatever they undertake, and the fullness of the Spirit alone does not remove the inaptitude and correct the defect.

It is not necessary, however, that any one should be destitute of wisdom in the management of either his secular or religious work; for it is written, "If any of you lack wisdom, let him ask of God, that giveth to all men liberally and upbraideth not, and it shall be given him." Nothing can be clearer than this. If any man among the saints, no matter who he may be, nor what the work to which he is legitimately called, finds himself lacking the wisdom for its management, he is ordered to ask of God and have his need supplied. If it be contended that the wisdom here promised has exclusive reference to the religious life, it may be replied that, granting this limited signification, the religious and secular are so intimately conjoined with a true believer that wisdom to live a happy and useful Christian life is also wisdom for true temporal interests, though a signal failure in the worldly view. It is, however, certain from this passage and other Scripture that all may have wisdom to certainly secure their own salvation and to be instrumental in saving others. "The wisdom that is from above," and which is urged upon all persons, "is first pure, then peaceable, gentle, easy to be entreated, full of mercy and good fruits, without partiality, and without hypocrisy." Hence all may have a wisdom which is "full of good fruits;" and it is surely a great shame for any church official to be destitute of it.

There are many among Christian workers who do not properly appreciate the element of wisdom in their qualifications, and who do not seek for it with appropriate earnestness. Indeed, there are some who scout the idea of caution at this point; they say, "Keep filled with the Holy Ghost and drive ahead; God will take care of you and all your blunders." Surely this is not scriptural counsel; it does not comport with the text and other portions of the word. We are, to be cautious that we proceed wisely with the work of God. It is true, we must not be so chary at this point that we will do nothing for fear we may blunder, but, looking earnestly for divine guidance, we should proceed with the work in hand, assured that under these circumstances the Lord will overrule our mistakes for his own glory and our ultimate good.

We see, then, from the Scripture under our present study, the divine ideal of preparation for Christian work in general and for church officials in particular. Honest report, full of the Holy Ghost, and wisdom, form a trinity of qualities which the head of the Church demands in all who fill her offices; and it is truly appalling that so many occupy these positions and are vainly attempting to discharge their functions without any adequate preparation, and, what is more alarming still, without any desire for it.

Here is an explanation of the general dullness of the modern prayer and class-meetings; the leaders are not aiming at the highest results of the Christian faith, and have nothing special to pray for, and the members have nothing new in their experience to state, and have little interest in stating over again what they have repeated many times. There is nothing progressive or aggressive in the religious life of either the leader or members to awaken interest. If both would arouse themselves and look into their great spiritual need, and shameful destitution of the necessary qualifications for their position and work, and would commence to seek with suitable earnestness the needed grace, the prayer and class-meetings would take on a radically different type. The question prominent with religious conventions and ministerial associations, "How shall we make our prayer-meetings the most interesting and attractive?" would find a solution. Let all aim at "honest report, full of the Holy Ghost, and wisdom," until they are reached; then aim to increase in knowledge, and love, and power, and continually walk abreast of the ever-increasing light of the Spirit, and soon the Church on earth would be in the stir and agitation of a happy revolution.

XXXIII
SEEKING GOD VERSUS HIS BLESSINGS

*Thus saith the Lord unto the house of Israel, Seek ye me,
and ye shall live: but seek not Bethel, nor enter into
Gilgal, and pass not to Beersheba; for Gilgal shall surely
go into captivity, and Bethel shall come to nought. Seek
the Lord, and ye shall live; lest he break out like fire in
the house of Joseph, and devour it, and there be none to
quench it in Bethel.* —Amos 5. 4-6.

THIS VOICE OF WARNING was originally addressed
to the Jewish people, but it comes with equal
emphasis to the spiritual seed of Abraham.
The members of the modern Gentile Church are as
liable as God's ancient people to miss the source of
all good, and, in their pursuit for a satisfying portion, seek it in persons, places, and things, rather
than in God alone. The text is, therefore, wholesome
counsel to all believers of all ages and all dispensa-
tions, as it guards them against seeking something
lower than God; something which, through wrong
teaching or a sad misapprehension of the nature of
their mistake, they are very apt to seek. In study-

ing, then, these words of precious caution, pass over, for the present, the positive command, and notice the negative but very expressive prohibition contained in the text.

"Seek not Bethel, nor enter into Gilgal, and pass not to Beersheba." The word Bethel means the House of God, and was the name given by Jacob to the place where he had his first revelation of unseen things. When he awoke from his vision he said, "How dreadful is this place! This is none other but the house of God, and this is the gate of heaven; and he named the place Bethel. In after years he built an altar there, and the place became the seat of the ark of the covenant during the troubled times of the Judges, and, at a later period, the home of the prophets and a center of popular worship sometimes true and sometimes false. These facts have led to a figurative use of the word to indicate sacred places, church relations, and religious experiences. Hence the words are guards against seeking the house of God, or religious associations, or spiritual experiences, as primary objects of pursuit. True, all should seek a home in the Church of God, all should seek the fellowship of the saints, and all should seek true experiences in grace; but these must be sought in God, and not apart from him. Many make the fatal mistake of substituting church-going and church work, and emotions excited by song and other religious exercises, for submission of the will to God and a scriptural acceptance of Christ as a personal Saviour. To such mistaken worshipers the order is, "Seek not Bethel," but make the visits to sacred places and religious assemblies, make church-going and church work, and make all the externalities of Christianity not the end, but means of the end, and that end seeking God.

"Nor enter into Gilgal." Gilgal was that place in Canaan where the Israelites pitched their tents after crossing the Jordan under the leadership of Joshua, and was so named because there the long-neglected rite of circumcision was administered, and the reproach of Egypt was "rolled away." There, too, they renewed the celebration of the Passover, and commenced to feed on the paschal lamb. There they commenced the use of the old corn of the land, and began to feast upon the milk and honey of the long-expected inheritance. The place continued a kind of head-quarters and base of supplies during the campaign for the conquest of Canaan, and in after ages was numbered among the sacred places of the Holy Land.

Thus Gilgal became a type of the incidents and early experiences in the life of holiness, a state of grace divinely symbolized by the land of Canaan. Hence the warning of this part of the text is against resting in the fact that the shame of former sins, of former back-slidings and former vacillations in the religious life, has been "rolled away" in the circumcision of the heart. It guards against resting in any former experience of feasting upon the Lamb of God, the "Great Antitype," or of resting in any former realization of what is meant by partaking of the old corn and wine, the milk and honey, and figs and pomegranates of the kingdom. Not a few of God's people, after passing from a state of partial to a state of entire sanctification, do not seem to feel the need of following on to know the Lord, and of making greater conquests in the realm of grace. Consequently they become enfeebled, their testimony stereotyped, their religious exercises perfunctory, and their labors inefficient. To all such there is eminent fitness in the admonition, "Nor enter into Gilgal."

"And pass not to Beersheba" is another part of the caution revealing a snare and danger much more subtle than any heretofore indicated. Beersheba was in the extreme south of Canaan, and was a typical word for the southern portion of that country. Hence the expression, "from Dan to Beersheba." In this south country Abraham, Isaac, and Jacob passed interesting parts of their lives. Here in the cave of Machpelah the bones of these patriarchs were put away; and here reposed the ashes of Sarah, Rebecca, and Leah. Here, to the descendants of these worthies, the sun shone more brightly, the air was more balmy, the soil more fertile, and the general configuration of the country more charming than any other land, and to it they would naturally turn for their ideals of home life and home comforts.

So, many earnest and useful Christians who never make the mistake of re-seeking their early experience in religion, nor their later experience in sanctifying grace, but reach after all their privilege in Christ, nevertheless, through satanic adroitness, get their minds on the sanctity of the fathers, or the peculiarly sunny experiences of eminent saints, and make these the objects of their pursuit. They unwittingly seek the blessings which God has seen proper to give other Christians, rather than God himself. They seek some ideals of saintliness which they have derived from the lives of others, and not God, as directed in the text. Their mistake is in an effort to "pass on to Beersheba." In short, the entire warning is to guard against resting in any grace already obtained, or coveting any past experiences, or reaching after any new and peculiar experiences, except only as these things may be the accidents of seeking more and enjoying more of God.

In closing, notice the reasons for the warning: "Gilgal shall surely go into captivity, and Bethel shall come to nought," and lest the Lord "break out like fire in the house of Joseph." In the present application of this scripture the meaning is that sacred places, visible churches, church relationships, early religious experiences, and every thing of the kind will come to nought. It means, also, that the grace which perfects the love of believers will not perpetuate their liberty, but leave them in weakness and bondage, unless they "forget those things which are behind, and reach forth to those things which are before, and press toward the mark."

Others, following on to know the Lord, have conceived that they could advance faster and please the Lord better by leaving their churches, breaking up old religious associations and forming new holiness alliances, holy bands, Christian unions, and the like; but fires of discontent break out and devour them. As the house of Joseph was a part or division of the Israelitish family, so these alliances are no doubt a part of the spiritual seed when they commence their operations; but seeking some ideals of holiness rather than God and the sanctification of his Church, they become discontented, jealous of each other, and a fire breaks out and devours, which there is no power in their faith and piety to quench. "Pass not to Beersheba, but seek the Lord, and ye shall live."

XXXIV
THE SPIRIT OF
WISDOM AND REVELATION

That God... may give unto you the spirit of wisdom and revelation in the knowledge of him. —Eph. 1. 17.

THESE WORDS CONTAIN one of the requests of the apostle Paul in a prayer for the Church at Ephesus, and open to view some points, now to be stated, which all believers should prayerfully study.

This petition was not for feeble Christians, or believers in a partially backslidden state. The apostle assumed them to be divinely illuminated persons, and addressed them as such, using the expression, "The eyes of your understanding being enlightened." The Greek text, both in the words and tense used, is still more expressive of a good religious condition. The literal rendering would be, "The eyes of your heart having been enlightened," the perfect tense being used for an emphatic present, or to convey the thought that their gracious state had long been a settled fact. The extent of their illumination and renovation he expressed in a preceding verse, where he says, "In whom ye also trusted, after that ye heard the word of truth, the gospel of your salvation; in whom also, after that ye believed, ye were sealed with the Holy Spirit of promise." In this statement the apostle allows that they had been illuminated by "the word of truth, the gospel of their salvation," which they heard; that, as a consequent of this enlightenment, they had trusted in Christ, and that "after they believed" and had received the grace which such belief and trust bring to the soul, they also "were sealed with the Holy Spirit of promise." Hence they were graciously adopted, they were sealed with the Holy Spirit of promise, and therefore, at the time of the prayer, were deeply experienced in divine things.

The apostle assumed that these believers were living up to the measure of their light, in the acknowledgment of God and the spiritual life which they professed. The expression, "in the knowledge of him," is rendered in the margin, "for the acknowledgment of Him," and the Greek will admit this translation. Moreover, the other requests of the prayer seem to demand this rendering, and make it highly probable that this is the Spirit's meaning in this place.

The burden, then, of the petition was that they might so acknowledge God as to demonstrate the divinity of their religion to the pagans and Jews around them. And in directing them in this acknowledgment the apostle guarded them against all Gentile vices, both of the flesh and spirit; he urged them to the practice of all the positive virtues in their social, church and domestic relations; he insisted that they should be imitators of God and keep filled with the Spirit; and, in short, that they should have on the whole armor of God; but makes no mention of oral confession. He speaks quite freely in the epistle of the working of grace upon his own heart, but gives them no direction about the verbal confession of their religious experience. He saw their great need to be purity of life, and saw this was the testimony needed by their Gentile countrymen. Hence he prohibited in detail the vices which they were liable to practice, and pressed upon them at length the graces to be manifested in their spirit and speech and demeanor. He emphasized especially the ethics of holiness.

The time has come in connection with the late revival of holiness to lay the emphasis on the same place. In its beginning, such was the backwardness in confession, that the leaders of the movement had to specially insist upon this duty. And those who faced the odium and made the confession, it was noticed, were specially blessed; their experience was made particularly clear, and they were empowered in a remarkable manner for their work. This greatly encouraged others to confess; and now it is so common that it has lost the power of crucifixion. At present the cross is found in the practice of the ethical system of holiness, and in laboring with suitable zeal for the salvation of others. The mere confession, after a proper consecration, is no longer attended with the entrancing views of Jesus and enrapturing experiences of a few years ago. Other means of self-abasement must be used. Self-denial in fasting and prayers, in giving and labor, and other sacrifices belonging to holy living are the present needs of holy people.

It is assumed also in this petition that, though these Ephesian Christians had deep religious experiences, they nevertheless needed "the spirit of wisdom and revelation for the acknowledgment of Him." They had the Holy Spirit in his regenerating and adopting work, and, being "sealed with the Holy Spirit of promise," they knew him in his purifying and empowering offices; but there were certain supernatural disclosures of truth and duty, and a certain divine prudence and sagacity in using truth and performing duty, yet needed; and for these the apostle earnestly prayed. It seems from this that the fullness of the Spirit, supplemented by a correct Christian life, does not raise the believer to the maximum of his power. He must have also "the spirit of wisdom and revelation."

There are other scriptures, too, which evidently hold out the same thought, that persons may have the baptism of the Holy Ghost and yet be destitute of the wisdom necessary for the work of God. A clear example of this is found in the Spirit's direction to the disciples in forming the polity of the Pentecostal Church. The order given them was, "Look ye out among you seven men of honest report, full of the Holy Ghost and wisdom, whom we may appoint over this business." A correct outer life with the fullness of the Spirit was not enough, they must have an additional qualification, they must be full of wisdom. And, as a matter of fact, have not all who have been consciously filled with the Spirit and have been called to active Christian work detected in their own earlier movements either too much rashness and precipitancy, or too much caution and compromise, for the highest and best interests of the work of God? Have not all such baptized persons, if ever they have become efficient in labors, had occasion to deplore their mistakes and ignorance, especially in their first efforts to spread the work of holiness? Is it not sadly true to-day that some, doubtless filled with the Holy Spirit, injure the cause which they try to serve by overlooking this pressing need in their qualifications, and, of course, by making no effort to supply the want?

Were "the spirit of wisdom and revelation for the acknowledgment of Him" more generally and deeply experienced by the professors of holiness, the work would take on new vigor and spread more universally and powerfully in the churches. "The spirit of revelation" would disclose to them their great personal weakness and utter need of divine aid, while the "spirit of wisdom" would lead to the steps necessary to secure the help; one would reveal in startling light the appalling condition of the great body of professing Christians, while the other would direct to such labor and zeal as would comport with the situation; the revelations of one would stir the heart to its greater depths, while the guidance of the other would protect from dangerous caution and ruinous precipitancy; one would disclose all the possible agencies, means and methods of such work, while the other would direct to the selection and arrangement of the most; efficient and thus the evangelism of apostolic times would appear again upon the earth. The suitableness, therefore, of the apostle's prayer for these times, as well as for his own day, must be apparent to all.

XXXV
LIFE AND LIBERTY

The law of the Spirit of life in Christ Jesus hath made me free from the law of sin and death. —Romans 8. 2.

As CHRIST IS the central figure of the Christian system, so to be "in Christ" is the central fact of Christian life. In the text, as in many other passages of the New Testament, the expression "in Christ Jesus" contains the reigning thought around which all the others of the passage move, and it ought to be well understood. A little further on in this epistle Paul speaks of us Gentiles as branches from the wild olive grafted into the tame olive, and thus symbolizes our union with Christ by the vital connection which takes place between the scion and the tree into which it is inserted. The Saviour, with still greater beauty and force, represents it by the union of the branch with the vine: "I am the vine, ye are the branches." Hence, to be in Christ Jesus is to receive from God the Father, through union with his Son, pardon, adoption, and spiritual life, known as *regenerating grace.*

Though every truly regenerated person has this living connection with his Lord it does not follow that the union is necessarily complete or perfect. A union may be vital and defective at the same time. Branches on the vine and grafts in the tree may have succulence and fruit on one side, while the other is shriveled and fruitless. Some insect or foreign substance has interfered with the articulation and prevents rotund growth and adequate fruitage. So, in the earlier and lower phases of Christian life, the divinely vitalizing power does not seem to permeate every part of human nature. Young converts, and indeed many old Christians, appear one-sided. Some are generous beyond their ability, but, though fluent in speech in all matters of business and social life, find it extremely difficult to pray, or testify, or do any thing in religious work requiring the use of the vocal organs. Others have no life on the benevolent side, and yet pray and testify with the greatest freedom and ease. In this respect their spiritual life, in some cases, is plethoric even to faultiness. Similar statements could be made with regard to other sides of Christian character and life. The union with the great Source of life is defective, and the development and fruitage incomplete.

When, however, under the light of regenerating grace, the believer puts away all self-seeking, all ambitious schemes, all worldliness, and whatever he judges to be offensive to God, and receives Christ for all he has engaged to do for the Christian, the union with his Lord becomes complete, and the Christ-life flows with all its fullness of light, love, and power. This is *divine renovating life in the measure of entire sanctification.* It is at this point that the believer becomes a Christian in the full New Testament sense, and, like a perfectly healthy branch, is filled with the succulence and fruit-bearing power of the True Vine.

In this blessed connection with the God-man the apostle

speaks of a certain freedom which is next to be studied. He calls it a freedom "from the law of sin and death." He speaks of two laws operating; one in isolation from Christ, called "the law of sin and death," the other, when in union with him, called "the law of the spirit of life." In the use of these words the apostle seems to have had in his mind the figure of the graft to which allusion has already been made. A branch cut from its parent trunk is brought at once under the law of death, and commences to wither and die. But if reingrafted before vitality entirely disappears its wilted appearance gives way to a healthy state, and it is delivered from the dominion of death. So, severed from Christ, the sinner is represented as dead, but, vitalized by a miracle of grace, and, perfectly grafted into the true Vine, he becomes completely freed from the domination and inbeing of sin. The Christ-life, entering his spiritual nature in full force, eliminates and expels the sinward tendency with which he was born. He is now "made free from sin, and has his fruit unto holiness and the end everlasting life."

In examining more in detail this freedom it must be noticed that it is from "the law of sin and death," only, and *not from personal peculiarities*. This is strikingly illustrated by the author of our text. Paul was a man of very strong convictions and unyielding purposes, and would be called in these times an obvious egotist. This trait was native to him, and did not disappear when he was filled with the Holy Spirit. More than twenty years after Ananias laid hands upon him, when writing his epistle to the Galatian Church, and speaking of the work of grace upon his heart, he uses these remarkable words: "I am crucified with Christ: nevertheless I live; yet not I, but Christ liveth in me; and the life which I now live in the flesh, I live by the faith of the Son of God, who loved me and gave himself for me." Now it is doubtful whether another statement, in so few words, and containing so much of the personal pronoun, could be found in any language, ancient or modern, living or dead. So we must not expect grace, even in its greatest plenitude, to deliver us from any of the constitutional traits that distinguish our personality.

The fact under consideration is of great practical importance, as it furnishes an extensive ground for a large charity toward those who profess entire sanctification, and as it also removes all occasion of fear that in obtaining this grace we shall take on any of the offensive idiosyncrasies of those who profess it. It neither takes away nor adds any of these things. It may bring to light in some characters personal peculiarities which have been hid from view, and modify those which have appeared, but it will neither create nor destroy them.

Again, it is not *a deliverance from any of the native appetites, senses, and instincts of the body, or any of the native propensities and passions of the soul.* Paul had "the fullness of the blessing of the gospel," yet found it necessary to "keep under the body, and bring it into subjection," lest he might "be a castaway." Paul does not speak here of the *sarx* — the carnal principle — which had long ago been crucified, but he speaks of the *soma* — the appetites, senses, and instincts of the animal man, and the propensities and passions of the rational soul. These he brought under grace, and, as the Greek word implies, into the service of the spiritual man. Instead of allowing them to lead into drunkenness, gluttony, resentment, and schemes of personal ambition, he made their gratification, in lawful measures and methods, the occasion of thanksgiving, praise, and the culture of longsuffering, gentleness, and other lovely graces of the Spirit. Neither may we expect a deliverance from any of these necessary elements of our humanity, but simply a complete emancipation from the carnal principle and its train of sinful affinities and promptings.

As space will not allow us to trace the relation of grace to all the appetites and passions, take for illustration of the whole subject the single passion of anger. This is, perhaps, with people generally, the most dangerous element in the structure of our humanity, and any manifestation of it the most difficult to reconcile, by those who have not closely studied the subject, with a state of entire purity. Yet, as a capability for displeasure at all sorts of wrongdoing, it is surely innocent and divinely approved, and sinful only when, under the control of depravity, it takes the form of ill-will and resentment. It was this form of it, no doubt, which the apostle had in his mind when he gave the order, "Put off all these: anger, wrath, malice, blasphemy," etc. God is said to be angry with the wicked, and even fierce anger is frequently ascribed to him. Jesus looked around upon a certain company "with anger, being grieved at the hardness of their hearts." And Christians are exhorted "Be ye angry, and sin not." Surely, then, the passion in question is compatible with the deepest experiences in grace, but must be watched with the greatest care. The same may be substantially said of all the appetites of the body and all the emotions and feelings which normally belong to our sensitive nature.

Lastly, this freedom is *not a present deliverance from all the effects or marks of sin*. Our apostle comes forward again for illustration. He was afflicted with "a thorn in the flesh, the messenger of Satan," and he prayed for its removal, but received as a satisfactory substitute, grace to cheerfully bear it. So, though "Himself took our infirmities and bare our sicknesses," we may not expect a *present* release from all our physical ills or all the mental disabilities which sin has entailed. The promise, "bare our sicknesses," is surely verified when grace enables the sufferer, as Paul, to "take pleasure" and "most gladly glory" in the affliction. This *is Christ in the sufferer*, bearing both him and his sickness and triumphantly filling the promise. Paul's experience, therefore, with his "thorn in the flesh," and his experiences with the sicknesses of others beloved by him, forbid the extreme view entertained by some on the subject of faith healing. He said of Epaphroditus, "he was sick nigh unto death," and of another, "Trophimus have I left at Miletum sick," and to Timothy, "use a little wine for thy stomach's sake and thine often infirmities," and gives no hint that their faith was at fault or that they suffered unnecessarily.

The salvation promised *now* does not involve the whole physical man, or we might at once dismiss all our bodily ailments and put on glorified forms. There is no reason why the phrase, "bare our sicknesses," should be strained to mean an immediate freedom from physical disease, while the phrase, "took our infirmities," in the same promise, is allowed to mean a gradual deliverance consummated at the resurrection. The truth seems to be, God has promised, under certain conditions, to strengthen us on the bed of languishing, to make our bed in our sickness, and, when it is best for us and ours, to heal us, either with or without medical remedies, and either gradually or instantaneously, as he may direct the faith of the believer.

So also, "by little and little," as beautifully symbolized in the conquest of Canaan, we get clear of the various mental and moral infirmities which destroyed carnality leaves behind. It is therefore highly important, both for the practice and enjoyment of holiness, and for a correct understanding of those who profess this grace, to properly discriminate between the disease of sin and the marks which it leaves. As one pitted by the small-pox carries about with him the traces of a former and very loathsome disease, but is now perfectly well, so one marked greatly by the sins of the past may now be entirely free from the leprous principle itself.

The freedom, then, brought to view in the text is emancipation from the "law of sin" — *Hamartia*— defined by Green in his Lexicon of the Greek New Testament, "principle or cause of sin," "proneness to sin," "sinful propensity." With the removal of this indivisible principle of evil all malevolence, resentment, and every other depraved affection disappears. For depraved affections are nothing more or less than excesses and erratic movements of the native and innocent passions under the domination of the carnal man. The old man crucified and cast out, and the Holy Spirit taking his place, the natural appetites, propensities, and tastes are tempered, put into their normal relations with each other and with the whole man, and, by gentle watchfulness and prayer, are easily held in their proper spheres. With this crucifixion there takes place also, in all cases where there is a scriptural apprehension of the believer's privilege, the entire removal of all abnormal appetites, such as the appetite for tobacco, opium, and rum. Thousands to-day, once enslaved by these perversions of the animal nature, now declare that grace has set them free, and utterly removed, so far as they can see or feel, all longings for these unnatural indulgences.

But, great as is this change, it is clear that no constitutional faculty or power, no God-given element of our complex nature, is removed or even lamed in its action. Nothing disappears in the work of entire sanctification but depravity and its brood of sinful affinities and affections, leaving the happy subjects of the grace in full possession of all their native powers, peculiarities, and æsthetical tastes. As scions from the gate, the greening, the bellflower, and other species of apple, grafted into the golden sweet and drawing their succulence from the same sweet trunk, bear apples of their own peculiar flavor, so believers united to Christ, and drawing their vitality from the same divine source, will each bear fruit flavored with his own personal peculiarities. Or, changing the illustration, as our clothing comes out of the laundry, cotton, linen, or woolen, as it went in, parting only with its impurities, so believers come out of the cleansing fountain as they entered, leaving behind all moral impurities and nothing more.

This gracious deliverance which has been the subject of our present study ought to be the experience of every Christian. To make it such it is only necessary for the justified believer, who is reaching after it with all his heart, in the spirit of irreversible self-surrender and acceptance of all the will of God, *to count it done*; not *has been* done, or *will be* done, but *is now* done while he is consecrating and accepting. God's order to such person is, "Be ye holy," "Be filled with the Spirit" — not take steps to be holy, or get ready to be filled with the Spirit, but BE *holy!* BE *filled!* The believer just described *has* taken steps; he *is* ready. What he has now to do when the divine voice comes, "Be ye holy," is to answer back, "*I receive, I am holy,*" and then and thereafter "reckon himself dead indeed unto sin, but alive unto God through Jesus Christ our Lord." This done, the soul will pulsate with the fullness of divine life, and shout the glad acclaim: "The law of the Spirit of life in Christ Jesus hath made me free from the law of sin and death."

XXXVI
Sin, and the Commission to Conquer it

Go, sin no more. —John 8. 11.

INSPIRATION FURNISHES three distinct definitions of sin. "Sin is the transgression of the law." "All unrighteousness is sin." "Whatsoever is not of faith is sin." These divinely-framed definitions take on deeper and deeper significance as the spiritual perceptions become more and more clarified. Unregenerated persons ordinarily see no wider scope for sin than the actual violation of the moral code of the Old Testament. To them sin means gross idolatry, blasphemy, Sabbath desecration, dishonor of parents, theft, murder, adultery, falsehood, and the like. By and by, as this subject is pressed by the Spirit upon the attention, they see that wrong-doing is not the whole of sin, but that it embraces also a failure to practice well-doing. They now discern sins of omission as well as of commission; but still their notions of Christian character are very immature. Its completeness, in their view, consists in the literal observance of the prohibitions and commands of the Decalogue.

Further on in the process of divine illumination, when the soul has yielded to the claims of truth and righteousness, and regenerating grace has been experienced, the domain of sin has so far widened as to encompass all unrighteousness; not only the acts of sin, but the state or condition of sinfulness. It now appears that it is not enough, important as it is, to break away from all sinful acts, and to practice all that is right, but much more necessary to *be* right. The soul now hears the divine voice, "Let thy heart keep my commandments," and cries out with David, "Behold, thou desirest truth in the inward parts." It now appears not only necessary to speak the truth, but to *be* truthful; not only necessary to deal justly, act mercifully, and practice all the divine virtues, but more necessary to *be* just, merciful, and possessed of a nature that is god-like.

When sin is removed from the heart, and the entirely sanctified state fully inaugurated, the domain of sin seems greatly widened, and the inspired definitions at the head of these lines take on still deeper meaning. Viewed from this stand-point any non-conformity to the higher and purer moral code of the New Testament offends God and contracts guilt. The rules adopted in this state, for the purpose of determining the purity of outward actions and inward states, are the self-forgetfulness and self-sacrificing love revealed in the New Testament, and practiced by Christ and his immediate followers. "In honor preferring one another," "We ought to lay down our lives for the brethren," Walk in love, as Christ hath also loved us, and given himself for us," and the like, are the touch-stones used to detect the subtler forms of sin in act and heart. Unless these become the rules of practical life, and their observance a spontaneity, it is known that the heart

is not yet attuned to the spirit of the new commandment—
a divine summary of the high moral code of the New
Testament dispensation.

Moreover, as spiritual light increases, and the finer
shadings of sin are discovered, the definition, "Whatsoever is not of faith is sin," has a special significance and
application. It is now discovered that actions in harmony
with the divine will and prompted by the purest motives
may, nevertheless, have a tinge of sinfulness thrown upon
them by a subtle unbelief. Members and friends of the
Church may feed the hungry, clothe the naked, endow
colleges, build churches, and aid in all benevolent enterprises, and yet indulge an unbelief that gives a sinful complexion to all their good deeds. Even prayers for what
God has clearly promised, uttered with a sincere desire
to obtain, may be offered without an expectation of receiving; and thus God is dishonored and the suppliant
confirmed in habits of unbelief. Many pray at the family
altar and in the church service for what they have no
idea of receiving, or, at least, they entertain doubts as to
whether they do or will receive. Thus the prayers of many
good and sincere people, when sifted in this higher light
of the Spirit, are clearly acts which confirm in habits of
unbelief rather than foster and strengthen faith. Christians should pray for only what they believe they may
receive, and pray till they receive. Thus they are not disappointed nor discouraged, and their faith is increased
and emboldened to ask more and more as the years pass.
"Whatsoever is not of faith is sin;" and whoever catches
a glimpse of its scope, and the many subtle forms in which
it may creep into the spirit and life, will not attempt a life
and state of scriptural holiness without utter reliance upon
the Mighty to save.

Notice, next, the order given concerning sin, or the commission to conquer it: "Go, and sin no more." The im-
peratives, "go," and "sin no more," express continuance

in activity. Many think that sin in thought, word, and deed, is a daily and hourly necessity during probation, and that nothing but death can overcome the dreadful foe. But the order is not, Go to the grave and end all connection with terrestrial life as a necessity to the cessation of sin; nor is it to cease business or an active life among men and retire into seclusion from society; but, Go to the nursery, to the workshop, to the counting-room, to the farm, or to whatever legitimate business has been chosen, and prosecute it upon the principles of holiness, excluding sin from every department. If the order under consideration were suitable to a fallen woman, with her associations and the snares that beset her, it is surely practicable to other classes of sinners.

Besides, the order "Go, and sin no more," coming from the Lord, means a complementary promise that the grace necessary shall be given for its execution. A business firm, sending out its agents, invests them with power to execute all business intrusted to them. Ambassadors sent to foreign courts to negotiate business and form treaties are clothed with the authority of the governments which they represent. God is not less liberal with his investments of power. When he orders "Go, sin no more," it is a divine commission to go into the business circles of this world and live a sinless life to represent his Son, to exhibit the salvation which He has wrought out, and to draw upon his almightiness for the needed help. To suppose such an order, without the expressed or implied promise of all necessary aid to execute it, would be a fearful mockery of the creature, and a view of the Creator which no thoughtful person could entertain.

It will be easy to execute the commission "Sin no more" when all love of sin is removed; when an abhorrence of it in all its forms enters the heart and the Holy Spirit takes possession of the entire man. And this is what is promised to the believer in both Testaments. A summary of these promises from the Old Testament is found in these words: "A new heart also will I give you, and a new spirit will I put within you: and I will put my Spirit within you, and cause you to walk in my statutes, and ye shall keep my judgments, and do them." In this is found not only the promise of purity, but grace to keep pure and obedient. So the New Testament furnishes a similar compend in the words: "Howbeit, when He, the Spirit of truth, is come, he will guide you into all truth," and, consequently, lead into no sin.

The text, therefore, must be viewed as a divine commission, tendered and pressed upon every sinner to abandon all sinful conduct, to divorce himself from all depraved affections, to cleanse his hands and purify his heart, and to elevate his spirit and life up to the highest and purest standard of New Testament holiness. Praise God for such a commission!

XXXVII
Supernatural Illumination

That ye may know what is the hope of his calling, and what the riches of the glory of his inheritance in the saints, and what is the exceeding greatness of his power to us-ward who believe. —Eph, 1. 18, 19.

THESE WORDS ARE SELECTED from a prayer offered for the Church at Ephesus, and contain requests for certain favors necessary to complete the happiness and usefulness of believers in every age. These Christians had been divinely instructed, "the eyes of their understanding had been enlightened," they had trusted Christ, having "heard the word of truth, the Gospel of their salvation;" they "also," "after that they believed, were sealed with the Holy Spirit of promise;" yet they needed clearer mental perceptions, as the Greek word used indicates, of the subjects named in the petition. They needed supernatural illumination upon,

1. *The hope of his calling.*— By this expression the apostle seems to mean the whole of salvation possible to

be known in probationary life. It would include, therefore, the soul's awakening, repentance, regeneration, adoption, witness of the Spirit, entire purification, growth in grace, and "change into his image, from glory to glory." Though these Ephesian Christians may have had great religious peace and joy in the Holy Ghost, and may have had correct general views of the economy of redemption, yet, like many Christians of this day, they lacked a divine insight into these different stages of the saving process, and their various relations to one another. This called forth the prayer under examination.

Many well-read, thoughtful, and richly experienced believers, and even some Gospel ministers, feel themselves disqualified to instruct others in the deep things of God, because they cannot clearly discriminate between the different phases of religious experience. They cannot discern well-defined lines between a true evangelical regeneration and entire sanctification, and fear to insist upon the latter lest they may confuse their weaker brethren, and be unable to lead them out of the confusion into the clear light. Others, again, not so thoughtful, impelled by holy love and an ardent desire to see their brethren in the enjoyment of full salvation, have taken the position of teachers without the qualification for which the apostle prayed, and, though they have led some into the experience of holiness, they have made sad work among others. So that the backwardness and inefficiency of some, and the temerity of others, make this petition as necessary for the modern Church as for the Church at Ephesus.

All Christians, and especially all Christian teachers, should be "sealed with the Holy Spirit of promise," and have this supernatural illumination upon "the hope of his calling." To this gracious state, and to this deep acquaintance with the process of salvation, God is calling both the ministry and the laity of the Church, and many of "the common people" are seeking and entering the experience. But, when they reach the fiery baptism, too often their pastors are not in a spiritual condition to understand them; they do not know how to instruct them; they counsel them to a course they dare not take, and thereby bring on collision and trouble. Soon those newly sanctified persons are found in some error of faith and practice, and holiness is charged with the mischief. But it is clear to any close observer, whose spirituality qualifies him to judge correctly in such matters, that the fanaticism found in some places among the professors of holiness, and the injuries done by some of them in other places, have been occasioned by the blunders of pastors in counseling and managing these persons. The great need of the times is a gospel ministry filled with holy ardor and divinely illuminated to lead forward the hosts-of God. Another matter upon which these Ephesian Christians needed clear light was,

2. *"The riches of the glory of his inheritance in the saints."* — Expositors of the Scripture generally view this inheritance objectively, as God's treasures of grace offered to the saints. But this is what is meant by "the hope of his calling," and would not be repeated in these words. A subjective rendering, making God to have a treasure in the saints, is a great revealed truth, one which all believers ought to clearly apprehend, and is the truth which, it is most likely, the apostle had in his mind in the use of these words. The Spirit gives it prominence among the great cardinal facts of revelation.

It is brought to view in the relationships which are used to express the nearness of God's people to him, as children and spouse. Parents have treasures in their children, as well as children in their parents. The bridegroom has a possession in the bride, as well as the bride in the bridegroom. So God has an inheritance in the saints, as well as the saints in him. He calls them his jewels, his crown, his portion. These words express precious treasure, great wealth, and that upon which the supreme affections are placed. God turns away from suns and stars, and all material creations with their glitter and brightness, and places his heart upon the saints as his treasure and portion. It will be noticed, too, that the language is keyed to its greatest tension to express the richness and preciousness of this treasure— "the *richness of the glory* of his inheritance."

The whole trend of Scripture is to the effect that God loves his trusting people with "an everlasting love," and has given to them both himself and every thing he has to give in earth and heaven; and he graciously asks them to reciprocate this affection. He represents himself as pining for the supreme love of his people, and as being unable to bear their refusal. Reason has often been dethroned, and numberless hearts have been broken by disappointed and thwarted love. So the Gracious One, reason must infer, woos the warmest and deepest affections of believers, not only to save them and make them supremely blest, but also to save himself from an infinite and everlasting heartache.

Such statements are a heavy strain upon the general faith of the Church, and lead most Christians to say with David, "Such knowledge is too wonderful for me; it is high; I cannot attain unto it." True, none can see God except the pure in heart, and to none but these, or those who fear him in this highest sense, can he disclose these wonderful secrets of his heart. "The secret of the Lord is with them that fear him; and he will show them his covenant." He will show them the love of his heart, and make known to them his proposal to join himself to them in everlasting union.

It will be clearly seen that such views of this wondrous theme, God's inheritance in the saints, as purified believers can bear and understand, and the Holy Spirit reveal, must greatly deepen spiritual fervor and intensify religious zeal. The subject, properly apprehended, inspires and comforts as no other theme can; it leads, as no other truth can, to the deepest submission and most willing offering of self and all to God and his cause. There was one more matter upon which light was needed:

3. *"The exceeding greatness of his power to us-ward who believe."* — These believers, like all who have been "sealed with the Holy Spirit of promise," already knew much of God's power to save; but there was a sweep in that power which they did not know.

The apostle discerned something of its greatness, and coveted the view for his brethren at Ephesus. He saw it to be the same energy which raised Christ from the dead and set him at God's right hand in the heavenlies; which placed him above all might and dominion, and every name that is named in this world, and that which is to come; which put all things under his feet, and which placed him head over all things to the Church. He saw it as a power that could put life into the dead, that could change the moral nature of responsible beings, and work other wonders beyond all the impersonal agencies of the material universe. He saw it as the substance of which all geological and astronomical forces are the merest shadows. He saw it as the living potency of which cyclones, earthquakes, volcanic eruptions, terrene castrophes [*sic*], stellar movements, and marshaling of suns with their systems of worlds are the feeblest pulses. He saw, therefore, no obstacle, except the creature's own unbelief, in the way of realizing the consummation of all God's marvelous plans of grace for his people. Hence he prayed that God would give these Ephesian Christians to see that, for this life, "He is able to do exceeding abundantly above all that we ask or think;" and, for the life to come, he is able to raise them from the dead, to place them with his Son at his own right hand, and bring them to the enjoyment of all that is meant by the "hope of his calling," and "the riches of the glory of his inheritance in the saints."

XXXVIII
THE REDEMPTIVE WORK
GENERICALLY STATED

*Happy art thou O Israel; who is like unto thee, O people
saved by the Lord!* —Deut. 33. 29.
*Therefore, if any man be in Christ, he is a new creature:
old things are passed away; behold, all things are become new.* —2 Cor. 5. 17.

A T THE TIME the first quoted words were uttered by Moses the people were not yet in
possession of their inheritance. They had
been delivered from bondage, had made the wilderness journey, were near the Jordan crossing, and
would sooner or later be settled in Canaan. Moses,
however, views them as already established in the
Promised Land, and breaks out in the language of
the text, "Happy art thou, O Israel; who is like unto
thee, O people saved by the Lord!" He speaks of
them as a saved people while they were yet in the
process of salvation.

This salvation embraced several great facts, comprising many other subordinate ones. It embraced the deliv-

erance from Egyptian bondage, the baptism unto Moses in the cloud and in the sea, the passage through the wilderness, with its lessons and discipline, the entrance into Canaan and seizure of that land, the celebration of the passover, and, finally, the victorious wars and the conquest of the country. These facts, some of them past and historic, and some of them at that time yet to transpire and predicted, are all grouped together and summarily presented in the words "happy" and "saved."

Let it be noted that all these facts, though embraced in the scope of Israel's redemption, were transactions distinct from one another. The exodus from Egypt was an event affecting the political condition of the people; a passing out of slavery into freedom. The baptism unto Moses was a change from the idolatry of Egypt to the worship of the true God, and affected their religious state. The wilderness travel, with its experiences, differed from what preceded and succeeded it. The entrance into Canaan was a transaction widely separated both in time and place from the deliverance from bondage, though both events affected their civil condition. Had Egypt and Canaan been contiguous countries the act of passing from one would have been a passage into the other, but they were separated by a wide extent of country. The circumcision and feast upon the paschal lamb were symbols of a much higher type of spirituality than they had ever enjoyed before. And, lastly, their successful wars under the divine leadership through Joshua, and their peaceable possession of the country so long as they were loyal to God, though depending on all the preceding facts as necessary antecedents, were, nevertheless, transactions radically different from all the others.

Another thing to be carefully noted is, that in all the statements made in these records, both by the Lord and by Moses, concerning Israel's redemption, the emphasis is laid especially upon the entrance into Canaan and the high type of spirituality which they were to obtain and exhibit in that land. When the Lord appeared unto Moses at Horeb in the burning bush, and announced his purpose to deliver his people, few words are used to express this deliverance, but many to express the more important matter of settling them in the land promised to Abraham and his posterity (See Exod. 3. 8). This is an instance of what is noticeable in other divine intimations of the same purpose. So, also, when the passage of the Red Sea was made, and Moses sang his song of triumph, he gave a large place to the prospective settlement of the people in Canaan. Even in this flush of victory he gives importance to the deliverance only as it was necessary to, and prophetic of, certain possession of the promised inheritance (See Exod. 15. 14, 18). The same sentiment is prominent in other sayings of Israel's great leader.

But not less was the emphasis which was placed upon the high type of spirituality that was to mark their religious life in that land. There they were to be "perfect with the Lord," there the Lord was "to circumcise their heart, and the heart of their seed," there they were "to love the Lord with all the heart, with all the soul, and with all the might," and there they were to observe the highest forms of civil, social, and domestic religion (See Deut. 6. 1, 9; 18. 9, 13:30. 5, 6).

Now these records are historic symbols of actual Christian experience and life under the New Testament dispensation. Paul settles the application of the symbols in his first letter to the Corinthians when he says, "All these things happened unto them for ensamples: and they are written for our admonition, upon whom the ends of the world are come."

These observations prepare the way for a similar exposition of the text selected from the New Testament Scriptures. "Therefore, if any man be in Christ, he is a new creature; old things are passed away; behold, all things are become new." The gracious state here brought to view, like happiness and salvation of Israel spoken of in the text from the Old Testament Scriptures, embraces several important facts.

1. To be in Christ, to be a new creature, for old things to pass away, and for all things to become new, comprise the abandonment of sin and the service of Satan, the removal of guilt and the impartation of spiritual life, the discovery of inherent depravity and utter inability to keep the law, the renunciation of this native evil and of every thing in practice that would foster the impurity, the acceptance of the Holy Spirit in his purifying and empowering work, and the entrance upon a course of continuous victory over sin and continuously rapid progress in grace. These facts in the process of salvation, often brought to notice specifically in the Scriptures, are here generically presented, as were the great transactions in Israel's redemption.

2. Notice, next, that these facts embraced in a complete deliverance from sin, though often joined in promise and prophecy and command, are nevertheless distinct transactions, and may be widely separated in time and place of occurrence. The abandonment of a sinful course, corresponding to the exodus from Egypt, affects the sinner's outer life. The pardon and regeneration which follow, corresponding to Israel's baptism unto Moses, affect the state of the heart, changing devotion to the world into the worship of God. The effort to grow in grace, the consequent discovery of inward defilement, and the necessity of a deliverance from it, corresponding to the wilderness passage, the giving of the law, the experiences at Kadish, and the lessons at other points, differ from all that goes before and comes after in the work of saving the soul. The renunciation of all that would feed the carnal life, and the acceptance of all that belongs to a state and life of perfect holiness, corresponding to Israel's aban-

donment of the wilderness life and passage across the Jordan into Canaan, and comprising the believer's consecration, differ widely from the penitent's submission. The acceptance of the Holy Spirit in all his fullness, corresponding to the circumcision and paschal feast, though it relates, like regeneration, to the state of the heart, raises to a much higher form of saintliness and likeness to God. And the life of constant victory and rapid growth, corresponding to Israel's successful wars and conquest, though dependent upon antecedent states of grace, differ greatly from them.

3. Finally, it ought to be carefully observed that, as the Old Testament Scriptures place special stress upon the settlement in Canaan and the high form of religion to be practiced there, so the New Testament Scriptures place their emphasis upon "the perfecting of the saints." Take a few samples illustrative of this fact. In his intercessory prayer the Saviour said, "I pray not for the world, but for them which thou hast given me." Again, "For their sakes I sanctify myself, that they also might be sanctified through the truth." Entire sanctification was their great need. He prays also for all future believers, or regenerated persons, that, "As thou, Father, art in me, and I in thee, that they also may be one in us; that the world may believe that thou hast sent me." The union of believers in perfected holiness was the reigning thought in this prayer, and the reason assigned was that it is the divine method of reaching and saving a perishing world.

The same sentiment has prominence in the apostolic writings. The supreme thought in John's epistle is the cleansing from all sin and the possession of the perfect love which will give boldness in the day of judgment. Peter presses the divine order, "Be ye holy," and urges his readers to give diligence that they may be found "without spot, and blameless." For the most spiritual Church of his times Paul prayed night and day exceedingly that he might see their face, and perfect that which was lacking in their faith. The burden of all his recorded prayers was the purification of believers, and the chief end of his preaching was to "present every man perfect in Christ Jesus." For this, he says, "I also labor, striving according to his working, which worketh in me mightily."

While, therefore, the New Testament writers attach due importance to every stage of grace in the process of salvation, they evidently place the greatest stress upon the entire sanctification of believers. In his letter to the Ephesians (chapter 4. 11, 12) Paul declares that all church officials have their appointments "for the perfecting of the saints." The success, therefore, promised to Christian labor must be reached by observing this divine order. Hence the marvelous victories won in the work of soul-saving by the pentecostal and early apostolic churches. Hence, also, the rapid spread of early Methodism, and the achievements of modern evangelism where it gives prominence to the work of holiness. Here, too, is found the secret of the shameful failure of so much labor in the pulpit and pew; the order of God is either slurred over or neglected altogether.

The passages expounded have been selected from the counterparts of the two Testaments. The former summarizes all the great facts that made Israel a happy people, and presents them in one word, "saved." The latter groups awakening, repentance, regeneration, entire sanctification, and every other work of the Spirit in the soul's complete deliverance from sin, and presents them in a compendious statement— a new creation.

He brought us out from thence, that he might bring us in, to give us the land which he sware unto our fathers" (Deut. 6. 23). "And you, …now hath He reconciled, …to present you holy and unblamable, and unreprovable in his sight " (Col. 1. 21, 22). Therefore, "tarry," "wait," "depart not," till endued with power from on high, and then "labor and strive to present every man perfect in Christ Jesus."

XXXIX
THE NEW COMMANDMENT

A new commandment I give unto you That ye love one another; as I have loved you, that ye also love one another. —John 13. 34.

THE SAVIOUR SAYS, "The words that I speak unto you, they are spirit, and they are life." The more we study the sayings of Jesus the more we are convinced that they are brimful of great meaning. The utterance of the new commandment opens to the view of well-instructed faith immense views of redemptive provisions. Whoever will study it closely will see in it the rising of a new sun in the spiritual heavens, and the consequent disclosure of new wonders in the redeeming plan.

Some few months before the giving of this new moral code, the Saviour hinted at a new order of things that was soon to take place when he said, "He that believeth on me, as the Scripture hath said, out of his belly (mouth) shall flow rivers of living water. (But this spake he of the Spirit, which they that believe on him should receive; For the Holy Ghost was not yet given; because that Jesus was not yet glorified.)" When Jesus ascended, and the Holy Ghost descended in pentecostal fullness, the new statute took effect, and has ever since crowned the ethics of the New Testament.

This new moral code addresses itself to none but truly regenerated persons; for no others can appreciate its high behests or aspire to the character and life which it enjoins. The only law of the kind which unconverted persons can appreciate is the moral code of the Old Testament, and not until this, as their school-master, has brought them to Christ, and they have become new creatures, are they ready for any thing so high and holy as the new commandment. The life of God once planted in the soul, and fostered by holy living until there is a thirsting for God, for the living God — the believer is then ready for the disclosures of the new commandment. These disclosures are:

1. *A new standard of love.* — The Old Testament required its worshipers to love each other as they loved themselves; no more, no less. Under this law the disciples of our Lord seem to have felt at liberty to dispute which of them should be the greatest in the kingdom of heaven. It is not revealed upon what ground the aspirants urged their respective claims, but it can be readily seen that one might claim pre-eminence on the ground of seniority, another on the ground of extra service rendered, another on the ground of natural fitness or acquired ability, another on the ground of conventional rights, and the rest from other considerations, all in harmony with the existing law of love.

After the new commandment took effect no such controversy could arise. This required them "in honor to prefer one another;" to give preference to each other in all matters of honor, preferment and happiness, and to love each other as Christ loved them and gave himself for them. The only controversy that could arise under the new order of things, concerning a matter of honor or position, would arise from each insisting that his brother should have it, whatsoever might be his own natural or conventional claims. If, however, the question were, Who shall bear the disappointments, the losses and other sufferings? each must insist on doing it himself, and, as far as possible, releasing his brother. "If meat make my brother to offend, I will eat no flesh while the world standeth, lest I make my brother to offend." Here is no division of inconvenience and suffering, but a voluntary and cheerful assumption of it all. The standard of love, therefore, under the dispensation of the Spirit, is not "as *thyself*," but immeasurably higher, *as Christ loved us and gave himself for us.* Another disclosure of the new commandment is

2. *A new model of human excellence.*— The Old Testament saints were ordered to be holy because God is holy, but it does not appear that they ever attained the idea of being "perfect, as our Father which is in heaven is perfect," or being holy as God is holy, or being *like God.* They had the divine promise, "I will walk among you and be your God, and ye shall be my people," but it was not until the new commandment was published that the Spirit revised the promise and put it into the more significant language of the New Testament, "I will dwell in them, and walk in them; and I will be their God, and they shall be my people." Toward the close of the Old Testament times there was an obscure prophecy that the day was approaching when "the feeble" among God's children "should be as David; and the house of David should be as God, as the angel of the Lord before them;" but it was reserved for the New Testament worshiper to see unveiled, for his personal imitation, the Divine Model of the new commandment.

The uncovering of this model of human excellence under the provisions of grace suggested resources in human nature, or moral capabilities in man, heretofore unknown, of receiving and exercising godlike qualities; it also suggested redemptive provisions that had not been clearly revealed in Old Testament teachings. It was known that "The wilderness and the solitary place shall be glad for them; and the desert shall rejoice and blossom as the rose;" that the time was coming when the order should be given to "strengthen the weak hands, and confirm the feeble knees. Say to them that are of a fearful heart. Be strong, fear not; behold, your God will come with vengeance, even God with a recompense; he will come and save you;" but the idea does not seem to have a place in the prophecies, that there were resources in humanity and redemptive provisions to make man like his adorable Saviour, and that he might be one with him in work and worship, in joy and sorrow, and in suffering and victory. Hence there was also a disclosing of,

3. *A new incentive to action.* — Under the Old Testament economy supreme love to God, and love to man equaling love for self, was the motive power. Impelled by this the ancient saints endured "Trials of cruel mocking and scourging, yea, moreover, of bonds and imprisonment." The New Testament worshiper has not only the stimulus of love to God and man raised to an altitude unknown to the ancient worshipers, but also the powerful stimulus of *being like the God* he loves and worships. This is calculated to excite regenerated humanity to the highest pitch, and furnish to it the mightiest incentive to effort after the high tender made to evangelical faith.

This love to God and man, coupled to the inspiring thought of being like God, explains the self-giving, the herculean labors, and superhuman heroism displayed by some of the more eminent saints in different ages of the Church: traveling over land and sea, wandering homeless and friendless among all kinds of people, searching after the most abandoned and dangerous of men, not to accumulate wealth or knowledge for self, but to spend and be spent for others; and doing this in the face of hunger and thirst, of cold and nakedness, of stripes and imprisonments, of stonings and death, and at the same time declaring, "I am filled with comfort. I am exceeding joyful in all our tribulations." This is an exponent of the mysterious force which Spirit-taught souls perceive and feel in the disclosures of the new commandment. There is also presented to the Christian Church

4. *An epitome of a new moral code.* — The moral code of the Old Testament was divinely summarized in the language, "Thou shalt love the Lord thy God with all thy heart, and thy neighbor as thyself." The New Testament moral code may be summarized much like it, "Thou shalt love the Lord thy God with all thy heart, and thy neighbor *more than thyself*; or as Christ loved thee and gave himself for thee." Now since Jesus has been glorified, and the Holy Ghost given in all his divine fullness, to love God with all the heart means much more, or a much greater degree of love than was known to the ancient saints. It means such love as may be experienced and exercised by souls purified by pentecostal fire, and "filled with all the fullness of God."

What is meant by loving one another as Christ loved us has its explanation in the life and labors of the Man of Nazareth. "For ye know the grace of our Lord Jesus Christ, that, though he was rich, yet for your sakes he became poor, that ye through his poverty might be rich" (2 Cor. 8, 9). Hence Christ's love for us led him to sacrifice the wealth and honor of heaven, to endure the poverty and shame of earth, and to suffer and die upon the cross that we might be rich and happy and live forever. The moral code of the New Testament, therefore, requires its worshipers to take property, and reputation, and health, and all the dearest rights, even life itself, and lay them down at Jesus's feet, and hold them subservient to the calls of humanity. Its language is, "Walk in love, as

Christ also hath loved us, and hath given himself for us," and "we ought to lay down our lives for the brethren."

This love to God which is awakened in the soul by the purging of pentecostal fire and the fullness of the Holy Ghost, and this love for others which holds life and all the dearest rights subordinate to the good of others, distinguishes Christian perfection from the perfection of religious character under the old dispensation. It is, therefore, a higher order of the life of God in the soul; and hence it is a mistake to hold up the Old Testament saints as finished models for Christians. It would be well did the mass of Christians imitate these worthies; still, however, the New Testament model is the Nazarene, and those who can truthfully say with Paul, "Be ye followers of me, even as I also am of Christ."

It may be said, in conclusion, that whosoever will study the new commandment in connection with the facts of truly converted life and experience will be abundantly satisfied that the purgation, the utter self-abnegation, and the fullness of the God-nature which are necessary to fill its high demands, do not come to us when born of the water and the Spirit, but succeed to a subsequent baptism of the Holy Ghost and of fire, and then only in its morning light and beauty, requiring time to develop into the brightness of its noonday power and glory. It may be said, also, that in view of the disclosures of the new commandment, the Church of the nineteenth century is yet in the rivulets of salvation, while she is beckoned forward by mighty Amazons and shoreless oceans.

XL
DEFECTIVE CONSECRATION

Will I eat the flesh of bulls, or drink the blood of goats?
—Psa. 50. 13.

THE LATE REVIVAL OF HOLINESS has called the attention of the ministry and laity of the Church to the necessity of entire devotement to God, and a great stir has taken place in late years upon the subject in all the Protestant Churches. In all religious assemblies the matter of entire consecration is freely spoken of as a Christian duty, and every pulpit in our land is calling Christian people to this religious exercise. The apostles of entire consecration have multiplied with such astonishing rapidity that no religious teacher is now found anywhere who does not insist upon this duty with great apparent earnestness. But unhappily, from some cause, the matter of entire purification, to which a scriptural consecration primarily points, is almost entirely overlooked. The devotement urged seems to be something expended in the externalities of religion and what is called Christian work; including fairs, festivals, and other labors of the modern Church. It is not directed first to inward purity and then to work divinely assigned to each saved worker, and is, therefore, not a scriptural consecration. Either because these religious teachers know no better, or because of inexcusable carelessness, entire purity is not pressed as the great and important necessity of Christian life and experience, and hence the consecration is radically defective.

There are thousands in the churches to-day who are never heard to pray, testify, or exercise in any way in the public worship, and who persuade themselves that the reason is they have no talent for such service, but that they have gifts for other exercises in the work of the Church. They are highly gifted in conducting sociables, regulating festivals, and gathering material for bazars, and all such secular work, and take these gifts, which may be exercised by all worldlings, as the evidences of spiritual life. A lady in the church expressed her deep gratitude that the Church, in her increasing light and aggressive movements, had discovered work in sociables, fairs, and so on, which she could do for the Lord, as she never had any gift for praying, speaking in class, or conversing with sinners about the salvation of their souls. Poor woman, she was a stranger to spiritual life; and this continuous call to consecration and work had not revealed to her the great need of her soul, but had driven her to more zealous efforts to make the bazar a success.

This alarming state of things in the Church of to-day seems to arise out of the unscriptural notion that the great matter with God, in instituting the Church and calling us to membership in it, was to get our service and our money. Consequently a feeble emphasis is placed on closet devotions and spiritual communion, while great stress is laid on endowing colleges, building churches, and carrying on the other enterprises of Christianity. Hence, also, the scriptural method of getting money is overlooked, and other methods substituted which are more likely to move the carnal man. The appeals for Christian work and giving, now made from our pulpits, rendered masterly by the justness of their ethics and the finish of their rhetoric, seem to have but little spiritual force, and fall on ears with no spiritual quickening. Nothing moves till some measure, either of speech or method, is adopted which addresses the sensual, the pride, the ambition, or other elements of fallen human nature. Thus the hearts of God's spiritual children bleed, and their cheeks redden with shame, as they read in the city dailies, and are compelled to hear announced weekly from the pulpits, notices of these measures of replenishing the treasury of the Church. This state of things would rapidly change, if all the leaders of religious thought and action would keep filled with the Spirit, and urge a consecration which looks directly to inward cleansing, and indirectly to service and giving. Let the internal state be right, and all that is outward will soon assume a scriptural adjustment; and no substitute for this order can be acceptable and blessed of God. And because this divine order is practically ignored the sad state complained of has been superinduced.

When God's ancient people had fallen into the condition of the modern Church of this day, He rebuked them in these tender words: "Hear, O my people, and I will speak: O, Israel, and I will testify against thee; I am God, even thy God. I will not reprove thee for thy sacrifices or thy burnt offerings, to have been continually before me. I will take no bullock out of thy house, nor he-goats out of thy folds: for every beast of the forest is mine, and the cattle upon a thousand hills... If I were hungry, I would not tell thee; for the world is mine, and the fullness thereof. Will I eat the flesh of bulls, or drink the blood of goats? Offer unto God thanksgiving; and pay thy vows unto the Most High: and call upon me in the day of trouble; I will deliver thee, and thou shalt glorify me." These people committed the blunder of supposing that God was after their property and work, and hence all they had to do was to attend strictly to the legal sacrifices of their flocks and labor, and all would be right. But God told them that he was not after their cattle nor their service, but he wanted their hearts, and had instituted these rites for the purpose of getting their affections, and when their hearts were not in them they were an abomination to him. He was wearied with offerings that made them no better. He wanted their thanksgiving, their affections, their loving approaches to him in their trouble. He wanted to see them changing into his own divine image and nature, and as they had no such aim underlying their offerings He "testified against" them.

The Holy Spirit is reproving the Church of to-day with the same questions. "Will I eat the flesh of bulls, or drink the blood of goats?" Do I need your money or your service? Am I dependent on your labor or funds? "Offer unto God thanksgiving, and pay thy vows unto the Most High; and call upon me in the day of trouble; I will deliver thee, and thou shalt glorify me." It is your heart I am after; and your discipline in all that is Christly has led to the institution of the Church and its ordinances.

The organization of the Church on a plan of benevolence was not to get the money of the worshipers, but to furnish them an opportunity to show and intensify their love for God and man, and to develop the self-sacrificing principles of the Christ nature. When, therefore, money is obtained to replenish the treasury of the Church in any other way than by free, voluntary contributions, the great purpose of the system of benevolence is defeated. This is true when the methods adopted are on the principles of strict equity; but when they have a doubtful moral bearing the purpose is not only defeated, but the system is prostituted to ruining, instead of disciplining souls for a happy hereafter.

The appointment of the ordinances of the Church was not for the purpose of getting the labor of the worshipers, but to help their faith to grasp the divine image, and to aid them to develop the divine likeness in their spirit and life. The Saviour said, "If any man serve me, let him follow me; and where I am, there shall also my servant be." This following and being where Christ is does not relate to place, but moral condition. Let the believer follow his Saviour to the cross, and submit to the crucifixion of the self-life, and enter, through faith into a state of inward purity which will place him in wedded union with the adorable Bride-groom. This is the Saviour's meaning, and to this blessed state a scriptural consecration looks as the great end to be reached. The order, "Present your bodies a living sacrifice, holy and acceptable unto God, which is your reasonable service," has for its sequence, "Be not conformed to this world, but be ye transformed by the renewing of your mind, that ye may prove what is that good, and acceptable, and perfect will of God." There is, therefore, a fearful omission of truth and duty by those teachers of Christianity who urge a consecration that expends itself in the mere externalities of religion and what is called religious work, and does not aim primarily at the sanctification of the nature. Yet, from the silence of many pulpits on the matter of inward holiness, this is the consecration preached, and all that is practiced by thousands of those who occupy the pews. O for some trumpet tongue to awaken the ministry on this matter, and start the pulpits to uttering the voice of alarm!

XLI
THE SPIRIT'S LEADINGS

He shall direct thy paths. —Prov. 3. 6.

THE LEADINGS OF THE SPIRIT IS a prominent theme of revealed religion and an eminently practical one in true Christian life. It has not, however, commanded that prayerful study which its importance demands, and is, therefore, poorly understood by the mass of professed believers. Even writers upon the doctrine and experience of Christian holiness have passed around it or slurred it over by a passing remark which has failed to give the reader any satisfactory views concerning it. Hence the subject has been so generally misunderstood, and so frequently perverted by incompetent teachers, as to injure many sincere inquirers for the way of life. In different ages of the Church numerous believers, through a misapprehension of the nature and mode of the Spirit's leadings, have been precipitated into serious error and folly. It is vital, therefore, that Christians have a correct understanding of this deeply-interesting and practical doctrine; and it is the earnest prayer of the writer that the Spirit of Truth may direct his thoughts and guide his pen in this humble attempt to aid the inquirer in reaching the truth upon this subject.

1. *The nature of the Spirit's leadings.* — It is a common notion that believers, under the guidance of the unerring Spirit, must make no mistakes, but be entirely free from all error. And, viewed from the divine stand-point, this would be the case were these leadings of that absolute nature which they would be if man were a mere machine, moving only as he is moved. From this point of observation all events under the absolute control of the Unerring One must appear in perfect accord with the great ends of creation, and man, moved in the same absolute manner, would move unerringly to the same ends. But from the human stand-point even these absolute and unerring movements would not always appear to men free from blunderings. Indeed, the Great Ruler does many things which the unaided intellect must view as unreasonable and absurd. Faith only can say these providences are wise and benevolent. The distressing drought of some seasons would be the occasion of severe censure if caused by any one — were the thing possible — who had been elected by the people to manage the weather. An official who would so manifestly contravene the notions of citizens could never have a re-election to the same office. The providence which sweeps away the nearly mature crops by devastating cyclones, as occasionally happens, does what the unaided human mind cannot readily reconcile with infinite wisdom. So believers, were they under this absolute leadership of the incomprehensible God, must often do what natural reason would pronounce absurd. But this is not the Scriptural view of the Spirit's leadings. They are not absolute and unerring.

Whatever may be the nature of these leadings, they must embrace and require the exercise of man's rational powers, and in no way supersede the use of his God-given faculties. These leadings must comport with every thing involved in man's accountability, the freedom of the human will, the moral agency of man, and his liability to err and exposure to sin. Probation does not end when the Spirit begins to lead the believer, but continues, whatever may be the gracious state, during the entire terrestrial life. By keeping in memory these plain facts, which all must admit, it will not be a difficult task to reach correct views of the divine leadership. Christians are to be divinely led, but with such exercise of their discretion and judgment as will justify them in saying of this guidance, as of every other part of their salvation, "We are laborers together with God." Christians are to be divinely led, but not so as to interfere with the freedom of their moral agency, or to raise them above the liability to fall into grave error and grievous sins.

It is at this point where some of the most devoted Christians wander into dangerous notions and fanaticism. They are divinely assured that they are under the leadership of the Holy Spirit, and they suppose that whatever appears right and proper to them is prompted by the Spirit, and ought to have the approval of their brethren, thus overlooking their own liability to mistake. And because the Church will not indorse their notions, which they regard as the teachings of the Spirit, they are forced into uncharitable views of their brethren; then into distrust and alienation, next into complaint and censure, and finally into spiritual indifference and shameful backslidings. Had they been impressed with their own liability to mistake, and the great necessity of carefully examining their impressions, they would have escaped these disasters. So gentle and tender are the divine promptings, and so free from every thing like violence, that the most spiritually-minded must proceed with great caution and prayerful study, or they may fall into grievous mistakes and shameful sins.

That these statements reflect the correct views of the Spirit's leadings may be seen by a mere glance at these leadings as they appear in the lives of the sacred personages of the Old and New Testaments.

Our first parents, in their original purity, must have enjoyed the Spirit's guidance in the highest possible sense compatible with probationary life; yet they blundered in listening to the tempter and sinned in yielding to his suggestion. And as redemptive provisions do not propose to raise the believer above man's original state, and out of the sphere of the erring into the realm of the unerring, we might expect to find Adam's redeemed posterity exposed to the same or even greater perils. Hence, the most exemplary characters of both Testaments, except the Man of Nazareth, have blotted their records with blunders, and some of them with sins. "Noah was a just man and perfect in his generation, and Noah walked with God," and was led by the Spirit— for walking with God includes this leading— yet he fell into an egregious blunder in the use of his wine. Elijah so fully walked with God that, like Enoch, he was translated, that he should not see death: yet he entertained views of his brethren more uncharitable than the facts justified, and did some things which "the Lord God of Elijah" had to reprove. Though "the heart of Asa was perfect all his days," and he enjoyed the Spirit's leadings, yet he did many foolish acts which no royal personage should have done, much less one ruling over God's people. The perfect man of Uz, like Moses, spake unadvisedly with his lips, through the provocation of others. David not only erred, but sinned; and thus we find associated with the Spirit's guidance in the old Testament Scriptures not only human infirmities, but shameful sins. It is not assumed in these statements that the Spirit led into these mistakes, but, in connection with the general experience of divine guidance, these blunders took place through inadvertency and human weakness.

An examination of the subject will soon reveal that, in the practical life of New Testament saints, divine guidance is substantially what it was among the ancient worthies. The disciples at the day of Pentecost were brought fully under the control of the Holy Ghost and enjoyed his leadership to the full extent of New Testament promises; yet Peter went to such extremes in yielding to Jewish prejudice and conciliating Jewish favor, that he carried away Barnabas by his dissimulation, and received a severe and just rebuke from the junior apostle. After this Paul, in turn, and Barnabas, his stanch friend and companion in travel, though joined in labor by a direct order of the Holy Ghost, so differed about taking John Mark with them, and so sharply contested the point, that they severed the divinely-appointed union between them, and each united with other companions in travel and labor. These instances are sufficient to show that the Spirit's leadings in the new, as well as in the old, dispensation do not supersede the necessity of carefully testing all notions, plans and enterprises; and, with all this, the most spiritual will make mistakes. "It is human to err;" and God will not lift believers out of the sphere of the human in this life. Let no one, therefore, who consciously enjoys divine guidance, rashly conclude that he is always right and that he should not listen to the counsel of others. That believer is already in the abyss of fanaticism, who thinks that he is so divinely led that he can make no mistake, and is unwilling to be instructed by his brethren and those over him in the Lord.

Before leaving this part of the subject it must be stated that the *purposes* of those who are led by the Spirit in all their arrangements and enterprises, however much they may blunder in the execution of their plans, point unerringly to the glory of God. As the hidden power which points the magnetic needle to the pole acts the same and constantly, however much the needle itself oscillates amid disturbing forces, so the impelling motives of all under the leadership of the Spirit act the same and constantly to the divine glory, whatever may be the disturbing influences about them. Any faultiness in the purposes would disjoint the moral relations and forfeit the divine guidance. The perfection of religious character demands perfect purity in the motives, but not perfect wisdom and correctness in the actions. Let no one, therefore, claim divine guidance who continues to indulge willfulness, or self-seeking, or ambitious schemes, and whose intentions cannot stand the test of the dying hour and the judgment day. Whoever is led by the Spirit, whatever may be his blunders in carrying out his intentions, is ready to live or die; he is ready for this world or any other world; he is ready for any thing which God appoints or permits; *he walks with God*. In short, the idea of infallibility which the mind intuitively connects with the thought of divine guidance must find its demands in the realm of the motives, and not in the execution of plans.

2. *The mode of the Spirit's leadings.* — In the awakening of sinners, the regeneration of believing penitents, and the entire sanctification of believers, the Holy Spirit, besides direct action, employs various instrumentalities. So in the matter of guidance the Spirit does not depart from the policy of using means in connection with direct impressions. Most of the scriptures promising divine leadings involve, either directly or indirectly, the thought of means. Take, for illustration, from the Old Testament the promises: "I will instruct thee and teach thee in the way in which thou shalt go," and, "Thou shalt guide me with thy counsel, and afterward receive me to glory." It will be noticed in these promises that believers are to be directed by divine instruction and teaching and guided by counsel; but this teaching and instruction and counsel

are to be found in the Bible. So the promises of guidance
in the New Testament involve the same thought of instrumentality. The Saviour said of the Spirit's teaching
(R.V.): "He shall bring to your remembrance all that I
said unto you," and "He shall guide you into all the truth;
for he shall not speak from himself." In these promises
the Spirit is to recall the utterances of Jesus, to guide into
"the truth" of revelation, and not to speak "from himself." Hence, according to both Testaments, the doctrines,
the precepts and the teachings of the Bible are the great
means employed by the Holy Spirit in directing believers. But the Scriptures do not furnish a specific rule for
every possible case, and, consequently, general principles
must be studied and applied in the absence of definite
instruction. This calls into exercise the Christian's rational powers, and makes him a "worker together with God"
in shedding light upon the narrow way.

Again, in determining duty in the various emergencies of life believers must, as occasion requires, consult
their feelings of propriety, their common sense, their reason, and all the faculties with which God has endowed
them. In the treatment of others they must respect the
feelings, the peculiar notions and even the foolish prejudices of those whom they would benefit. The practical
workings of these principles may be seen in the course to
which Paul was led by the Holy Spirit in his evangelistic
labors. He said, "I please all men in all things, not seeking mine own profit, but the profit of many, that they
may be saved." Again: "Unto the Jews I became as a Jew;
to them that are under the law as under the law; to them
that are without law as without law; to the weak became
I as weak; I am made all things to all men, that I might
by all means save some." These statements are not to be
so interpreted as to make Paul compromise, in any degree, the great principles of the Gospel, but as yielding,
for the good of others, his own preferences, tastes, conve-

niences, and comforts, so far as compatible with the purity of Christianity. Thus it will be seen that Paul's course was the simple dictate of reason and common sense, and had not only the sanction of his Lord, but contained also his divine guidance. In other words, Paul's judgment and the Holy Spirit co-operated in directing his labors among the people, and hence he could truthfully say, "We are laborers together with God."

Another factor in this guidance is the counsel of brethren, and especially those over us in the Lord. The divine command is: "Ye younger, submit yourselves unto the elder; yea, all of you be subject one to another;" thus teaching that the Spirit leads the younger through the counsels of the elder, and the elder through the suggestions of the younger. Another order is: "Obey them that have the rule over you, and submit yourselves," or, as it reads in the margin: "Obey them that guide you." Hence, it is infallibly certain that one of the means used by the Holy Spirit in leading believers is the advice and instruction of spiritual leaders chosen from their own number. The godly counsels, therefore, of church officials cannot be ignored without incurring the divine displeasure.

It must not be forgotten, however, that there always will be enough of human infirmity in the counsels of the Church to necessitate attention to the apostolic admonition, "Prove all things; hold fast that which is good." This is God's arrangement; and it is an important part of human trial to sift truth from error. But when a church has so far fallen that her counsels can no longer be heard she should be abandoned; but let not every one who discerns the need of reform conclude that the time has come for separation, neither let him hasten to join any self-constituted reformer. Such precipitancy has ruined many sincere persons. When the proper time comes God will provide a Luther or a Wesley for the emergency, and authenticate his mission in some way to Christian people.

Divine providence, as manifested in the course of events, must not be overlooked by believers in settling the question of duty on many occasions and in many emergencies. But this source of instruction must be consulted with the greatest care and closest discrimination. It is easy to discern that the Spirit will not lead to what the course of events renders impossible; but how much difficulty the Spirit would have the Christian encounter and overcome to carry a measure, or what degree of providential favor he must have to assure divine approval in a given course, are matters not so easily settled. Much apostolic labor was performed and success achieved under the promptings of the Holy Spirit, but in the face of unfriendly providences. On the other hand, following encouraging indications has not always been the safe and prosperous course. Finding a ship at Joppa ready to sail for Tarshish appeared to Jonah a very favoring providence, but the divine pointing was in an entirely different direction. The marvelous providence which placed Moses in the family of Pharaoh, which educated him in all the wisdom of the Egyptians, and gave him unlimited influence in the imperial court, could have been easily interpreted to mean that he should remain in this brilliant and luxurious circle, and use his large influence to better the civil condition of his enslaved countrymen. The Holy Spirit, however, pointed to a lengthy pupilage in the flesh-subduing solitudes of the wilderness, preparing him, not to better the enslaved condition, but to emancipate and settle in the land of promise these children of Abraham. Thus, apparently favoring providences and the Spirit do not always point in the same direction, neither do apparently adverse providences and the Spirit always point in opposite directions. Hence, the inferences from the course of events must be made with the greatest caution; nevertheless, they must be made, at times, in determining the course to be pursued.

Finally, the Spirit leads by direct impressions upon the heart. He has promised to change, to purify, to dwell in believers, to fill them with holy emotions and impulses, and to draw them to a life of loyalty to God. But mere influences and impressions, however holy, are not safe forces without proper guidance. The little boy under the pure impulse of filial affection, but controlled by boyish instinct and judgment, wastes the money which has been given to him in purchasing a hobby-horse for his father's birthday present. Had he consulted his mother or the older children he would have bought something useful, and a present suitable to his father's age and tastes. So, many saintly men and women, moved by holy impulses but directed by their own crude notions, have wasted the grace of God in silly and unprofitable action. Had they consulted their brethren, and gathered instruction from the Scriptures, they would have blessed others and saved themselves from shame. It is recorded that certain disciples at Tyre "said to Paul through the Spirit, that he should not go up to Jerusalem;" and when he reached Caesarea, "they of that place besought him not to go up to Jerusalem;" but Paul, with broader views of his mission than they had, could not accept their counsel, notwithstanding it was given "through the Spirit." "And when he would not be persuaded," says the narrator, "we ceased, saying, The will of the Lord be done." Thus one party, moved by the Holy Spirit, dissuades; the other, moved by the same Holy Spirit, but with more comprehensive views, persists in his course. The first party then concludes itself in error and accepts Paul's course as the right one. It would certainly be a great blessing to the Church had all Christians such correct views of holy impulses, pure impressions, the Spirit's leadings, and their own fallibility under these leadings, and were they as willing to be corrected upon presentation of suitable information. This would be the case did believers study the subject as they ought.

It is hoped that what has been written is sufficient to

lead the reader to see that the infallibility which the mind intuitively associates with the Spirit's leadings is found in the domain of the intentions and not in the execution of plans, and that the method of leading is not wholly by inward impressions, but by the light which the believer gathers from these impressions and all other sources of information. As men are "laborers together with God" in their conversion, their purification, and in the support of their bodies, so in getting light upon their path. God has promised to feed the faithful, but this includes their plowing and sowing, their reaping and gathering, their thrashing and winnowing, their grinding and bolting, and their kneading and baking. So the promise of guidance includes a close attention to the opinions and counsels of others, a careful study of the pointings of providence, a prayerful notice of inward impressions, a devout study of the word of God, and an impartial testing of all these notions, counsels, pointings and impressions by the Holy Scriptures, and a following of the best light thus obtained. Whoever does this will feel assured that there is answered in his experience the prayer of the poet:

"I want the witness, Lord,
    That all I do is right."

XLII
GROWTH IN GRACE

But grow in grace. —2 Pet. 3. 18.

ITS NATURE

GROWTH IS THE PROCESS of increasing the dimensions of something already existent and capable of enlargement. In the vegetable and animal economy it is an enlargement of size by the gradual assimilation of new matter by the living organism. In its application to things spiritual, as the intellectual and moral qualities of man's nature, it means an increase of their power and clearness of manifestation brought about by processes suited to the nature of such qualities. Now the natural way of increasing the retention of memory, the keenness of perception, the accuracy of judgment, or of improving any mental and moral quality, is exercise. And the Scriptures, in ordering Christians to grow in grace, evidently assume that the graces of the Spirit are, in some respects, subject to the same laws, and require the same process in their development. Hence growth in grace may be defined as the gradual unfolding and maturing of the divine life in man by the exercise of love, peace, joy, long-suffering, gentleness, goodness, and the other graces of the Spirit, upon their appropriate objects and occasions.

It must not be understood, however, that the exercise of the graces alone will unfold and develop the spiritual life. Strength of muscle is the product of a plentiful supply of nourishing food added to muscular exercise. The fiber and substance of muscle are derived from the food, and its strength from exercise. Eating alone, while it supplies material for fiber, will not give strength. And exercise alone, without food, will be succeeded by feebleness and decay. Food and exercise are both necessary. So a Christian may be ever so active in all the departments of religious labor and grow as lean as the kine in Pharaoh's dream; and thousands are making this mistake and suffering this result. So also a Christian may read the Bible and pray ever so much in the closet, if he do not exercise his love, peace, joy, and other graces in response to the calls of suffering humanity, he will be without strength. And many very devout Christians are without strength because they never exercise as they should in the work of happifying and saving others. He only who is devout, reads the Bible, and communes with God, who preserves a vital union with Christ, and who exercises his Christian graces in the work of God and bears fruit to his glory, will be a strong and growing Christian. Devotion and activity are both necessary and included in religious growth.

There is another fact to be carefully studied in connection with this subject. There is no power in growth to create or destroy, to bring into being or remove from being. It has to do with things already in being. It holds together, it binds, it assimilates, it increases, but never destroys, removes, or eliminates. Elimination and growth may take place at the same time in the same organism, but by radically different forces. Disease is not removed from the animal economy by a growth of the animal functions, but by medical remedies, or by some eliminating power in the system coacting, it may be, with the power of growth, but radically different from it. Weeds are not eradicated from among the useful vegetables by any form of growth, but by a specific act of the gardener. Inattention to this fact, involved in the nature of growth, has led many persons to believe that an increase in the power and efficiency of the Christian graces, implanted in the heart at conversion by the Holy Ghost, gradually overcomes and ultimately destroys the heart's inherent tendencies to wrong doing. But this view is at variance with the very nature of growth. An increase in the volume and power of the spiritual life would, logically, more easily control these tendencies, but make no approach toward their removal. But when we remember that these tendencies are indigenous to the soil of the heart, and, as a fact of experience, grow more rapidly than the graces, the longer continued the effort to grow into purity the more piercing the wail, "O, wretched man that I am! who shall deliver me from the body of this death?" Neither philosophy nor the Scriptures justify the notion that heart impurities are removed by any growth of the graces, but by a specific act of the Holy Ghost in response to the prayer of faith. It is the voice of reason as well as revelation that the very God of peace sanctifies wholly, that he creates the clean heart and renews the right spirit, that he purges with hyssop and makes clean, that he washes and makes whiter than snow, and that, too, by supernatural methods, and not by the natural processes of growth. Let no one, therefore, indulge the vain hope of getting clear of depraved tendencies by cultivating the graces of the Spirit.

There are some other facts in the nature of growth that might be examined at length, but will be brought under one general glance. The growths of nature are generally impalpable and unseen processes, the effects of which can only be seen after considerable lapses of time. Some of them are suspended for long seasons while the organisms undergo hardening processes, as vegetable growths during the winter seasons. There are other forms of growth which do not proceed by gradual and uniform advances, but by sudden bounds at irregular intervals, as the growth of nations by the accessions of new states at different periods of their history. The progress and development of spiritual life seem to partake of all these forms of growth. It is generally undiscernible except at considerable intervals; it seems at times and under some circumstances to be suspended, but, like vegetation during the winter, is gathering force for resilience and greater development in the future. Sometimes, under superior teaching, and at seasons of special outpourings of the Spirit, believers experience sudden uplifts to higher planes of light, love, and power, than ever known before.

But whatever may be the peculiar form or phase of the growth, it must always be referred to what the Spirit has already implanted in the soul, and not to what the Spirit has yet to do in eliminating and removing depravity. It is vital to every Christian to have correct notions on this subject. Mistaken views upon this matter, giving rise to mistaken action, may be followed by a painful and life-long struggle with inbred sin. Correct views, followed with appropriate action, will end the struggle in a moment, by the power of the Holy Ghost in response to one simple act of faith.

Its Conditions

The word "growth" is borrowed from the material world, and is used in the sacred vocabulary to signify a spiritual phenomenon resembling the growth of living organisms. Hence we must come to these living organisms and study their increase and development, to see the meaning of growth in its application to spiritual qualities. In studying the conditions of vigorous growth in vegetable nature we discover that a fertile soil, plenty of rain and sunshine, and a freedom from noxious plants, are indispensable prerequisites. In the animal kingdom we discover the prerequisites to be an abundance of wholesome food, keen appetite, an unimpaired digestion and assimilation, or freedom from physical disease. We learn, therefore, that a rapid and vigorous growth of the graces requires that the soil of the heart be properly prepared by a genuine repentance, that there be an abundant effusion of the Spirit and sunshine of gospel promises secured by earnest prayer and careful reading of the word, and that all the noxious growth of pride, worldliness, and other depraved affections be removed from the heart. Or, borrowing the similitude from the animal economy, there must be plenty of nourishing food, "the sincere milk of the word," and the "strong meat" of the Gospel, a keen appetite or relish for spiritual things, and an avidity in appropriating and using gospel truth. This divinely-chosen method of representing Christian progress teaches, therefore, what is confirmed by universal Christian experience, that a necessity to strong and vigorous religious growth is a clean heart, or a heart freed from all spiritual disease. Spiritual uncleanness and disease will interfere with religious growth as noxious weeds and physical disease, will interfere with growth in the vegetable and animal organisms.

There may be a feeble and sickly growth of vegetation in poor soil, with little rain and sunshine, and amid encumbering weeds; and there may be a feeble animal growth upon poor diet, with a dull appetite and impaired digestion. So also there may be a sickly growth of the Christian graces under similarly unfavorable circumstances; but this is not the growth that a Christian should desire, nor is it the growth enjoined in the Scriptures. God has provided and revealed something better, and has ordered all believers to "Be strong in the Lord and the power of his might." No one has a right, therefore, to remain in spiritual feebleness or take any step that will protract such a state, but is under the most solemn obligation to place himself upon the conditions of the most rapid and vigorous religious development. Hence he should seek, as a primary necessity for Christian growth, a clean heart, or the removal of all disease from the spiritual nature. If he do not he may read and study, pray and supplicate, work and toil, attend all the conventions for religious purposes, go to all the camp-meetings far and near, and still he will be without strength. The spiritual disease within will neutralize all this devotion and activity. This is more than intimated by inspired teaching.

Peter may be denominated the great apostle of growth. To him all the advocates of a growth into holiness appeal in the advocacy of their theory. But they fail to correctly interpret this apostle. In the orders which he gives the churches to gradually advance in religious life he assumes that purity is an antecedent necessity. In his second epistle, chap. I, verses 5 and 6, he says: "And besides this, giving all diligence, add to your faith virtue, and to virtue knowledge, and to knowledge temperance, and to temperance patience," and so on. This has been interpreted to mean a gradual advance in the religious life until a state of perfected purity be reached. But a little care will discover that the apostle is urging a spiritual development which succeeds to, or follows after, entire purification. "Besides this," he says, "giving all diligence, add to your faith virtue, and to virtue knowledge," etc. Now let it be inquired, besides what? The answer comes in the preceding verse: "Whereby are given unto us exceeding great and precious promises; that by these ye might be partakers of the divine nature, having escaped the corruption that is in the world through lust." Hence, "besides this" means besides having the divine nature, and besides being freed from the carnal nature, "add to your faith virtue," and so on— that is, develop and mature the state of purity.

In the famous order of this apostle by which he closes his second epistle, "But grow in grace, and the knowledge of our Lord and Saviour Jesus Christ," he assumes that the persons addressed were "steadfast," or already in a favorable condition for vigorous growth, as appears from the preceding verse. Before he gave this order he gave another, which he viewed as antecedent in the order of grace: "Be diligent that ye may be found of him in peace, without spot, and blameless." Peace, spotlessness, and blamelessness first, then Christian growth and development. Hence the orders to grow in grace, or to advance in Christian life, is generic, and involves the more specific orders to be holy, to be perfect, to be strong, etc. To flee, therefore, to the inspired, or scripture orders to grow in grace, for the purpose of escaping the obligation to seek perfected holiness at once and now, is to misinterpret them and practice self-delusion. Cleared of this sophism and correctly interpreted these scriptures intensify the obligation to be holy now, and render more audible the voice which calls to present and perfected purity. The landowner who orders his tenant to grow for him certain vegetables includes in that order to properly prepare the ground and keep it free from weeds. So the order to grow in grace includes all that is necessary to rapid and vigorous growth, and to an athletic spiritual life— it is an order to seek the removal of all depraved affections which antagonize growth, and the possession of a moral condition favorable to it, in short, a state of inward purity.

Its Methods

There is no such thing as growing *into* grace. Grace once communicated to the soul, there may be a growth *in* it. Hence growth in grace presupposes an antecedent impartation of spiritual life to the soul by the Holy Ghost; and growth is the gradual enlargement and unfolding of that life. The methods of such development, from what has already been said upon the nature and conditions of growth in grace, will be easily pointed out.

I. *The adjustment of the entire life to a gracious state.*

As soon as the penitent seeker of salvation finds himself in possession of the graces of the Spirit he should call them into exercise in all the departments of life; he should commence to live a strictly religious life in every thing. He should commence to treat and use himself and all his powers as belonging to God. He should adjust his home life, his social relations and treatment of his fellows, his business habits and principles, and every department of private, domestic, social, civil, and religious life, to suit his new moral and spiritual state. In doing this he will discover in his nature something that opposes a life of uninterrupted devotion and spotless purity. Hence another essential matter in Christian progress is,

II. *The attainment of a clean heart.*

As soon as the young convert detects any impurity remaining in his spiritual nature he should, without any delay, fly to Christ and commence the plea, "Create in me a clean heart, O God, and renew a right spirit within me," and continue with unyielding purpose until conscious cleansing takes place. This discovery of remaining depravity, or antagonism to the ways of God, is a divine call to a state of entire purity, as the next necessary step to further progress in the divine life. Willful neglect, or disobedience at this point of experience, will not only prove a bar to further progress, but will turn the believer back to a barren, unsatisfactory, and wilderness life.

A refusal to go forward, when the borders of the promised land were reached at Kadesh-barnea, turned ancient Israel back into the wilderness to wander, suffer and die. So a failure to go forward, when the necessity of a clean heart has been discovered, has turned thousands of Christians back to a state of religious formalism and death. There is no safety at this point but in seeking entire sanctification! It is necessary to further progress, and hence is but one of the early

XLII: G<small>ROWTH IN</small> G<small>RACE</small> **275**

steps of the Christian's life-long work of growing in grace. A complete deliverance from all carnality being experienced, the believer is now ready for an untrammeled exercise of the graces and for rapid and symmetrical development. Hence, the next method to be observed is,

III. *A devotional exercise of all the graces.*

Intercommunion and fellowship with God is indispensable to any religious advancement. The Christian may labor and drudge at all manner of good works, until he sinks under sheer exhaustion, and grow leaner and leaner every day, unless he feed his soul constantly upon the bread which comes down from heaven. But, possessed of a clean heart, and continually communing with God, the believer will increase his love by deeds of benevolence, especially in helping and caring for the ungrateful and repulsive. His joy will be increased by devoutly looking on the bright side of every thing, and by obeying God in rejoicing evermore. He will develop his patience, meekness, and such graces by bearing, without murmuring, all losses, sicknesses, and other afflictions. His longsuffering, gentleness, and the like, will be enlarged in their volume by patiently enduring the insults and wrongs of others, returning to them good for evil, and doing all that can be done to reform and make them happy. Similarly all the other graces must be exercised.

Care must be taken that no one or a few of the graces be exercised and the others neglected. Symmetrical development requires that all the graces be brought into activity as providences and opportunities call for them. There is danger of Christians, even the entirely sanctified, running off on some favorite line of action and not being "fruitful in every good work." Such a course will develop religious malformations and unbalanced Christians. It is to be feared that many calling themselves Christians are cultivating some moral excellence or lovely trait in the character, and calling it growing in grace, while it is nothing more than willfulness or will-worship in some of their protean forms. One, for instance, has established the habit of church-going, has learned to pray fluently, and speak of shortcomings with propriety, and calls it growing in grace, while he gives little or nothing to benevolent purposes, hoards away money, and is known among traders as an unusually shrewd dealer. Another gives liberally, is reputed honest in all his dealings, goes to church regularly, seems to be interested in all church enterprises, and calls this growing in grace, while he seldom prays, gets out of temper, and indulges other depraved affections. These, so far from being growths in grace, are growths of covetousness and greed, of selfishness and formalism. To escape such spurious growths, liable to be mistaken for religious advancement, there must be a continual turning away from all sin, inward and outward, and a scrupulous and devotional exercise of all the graces of the Spirit.

Besides these general methods, necessary for and suited to all Christians, each believer will have some prudential arrangements and rules for religious culture and progress suited to his own peculiar condition and environments. These personal expedients will readily suggest themselves to the mind of every believer earnestly inquiring for the best methods to advance his spiritual life. But whatever notions may be entertained of the nature of growth in grace, whatever plans may be devised and rules adopted by private Christians for holy living, and whatever methods may be employed by churches for spiritual culture, they are all radically defective unless the reigning idea be, from first to last, holiness of heart, holiness of heart now, holiness of heart a present, future, and everlasting necessity.